D1496921

THE SCOTCH COMEDIANS

Also by ALBERT D. MACKIE

POEMS IN TWO TONGUES

A CALL FROM WARSAW

SING A SANG O' SCOTLAND

EDINBURGH

THE BOOK OF MACNIB

THE HEARTS

GENTLE LIKE A DOVE

EDINBURGH: AN INDUSTRIAL HISTORY

A TALE OF TWO BRIDGES

SCOTTISH PAGEANTRY

DONALD'S DIVE

THE
SCOTCH COMEDIANS

FROM THE MUSIC HALL TO TELEVISION

ALBERT D. MACKIE

STIRLING
DISTRICT
LIBRARY

THE RAMSAY HEAD PRESS · EDINBURGH

792.092
MAC

© Albert D. Mackie 1973

First published in 1973 by
The Ramsay Head Press
36 Castle Street
Edinburgh EH3 7AF

Printed in Scotland by
Macdonald Printers (Edinburgh) Limited
Loanhead, Midlothian

Acknowledgements

The author acknowledges indebtedness to the theatrical columnists: the three Gordons—Hislop (*Scottish Sunday Express*), Irving (*Daily Record*) and Reed (*Scottish Daily Express*)—the ubiquitous Jack House (*Scottish Field*, etc.) and Georgie Wood (*The Stage*); and to *Who's Who in the Theatre*. Also to Alec Finlay, Johnny Beattie, Rikki Fulton and other forthcoming members of a remarkably shy profession.

For finding, providing or allowing to use photographs thanks are due to Eric Popplewell of the Gaiety Theatre, Ayr; the management and box-office staff of the King's Theatre, Edinburgh; Charles McCorry of *Scotland's Magazine*; Miss Sadie Aitken; Mrs Armstrong of the Edinburgh Room, Edinburgh Public Libraries; R. R. Inglis; Grampian Television; and BBC Scotland.

Contents

Illustrations

The
Clan MacClown

A CASUAL observer of the Scottish entertainment scene might be excused for believing that once upon a time there was a wee man in a kilt called Harry Lauder and that he spawned a race of people called Scotch comedians. In fact, Lauder was not a typical Scotch comedian. He was the one who had most success abroad and his triumph led to a flood of imitators who waddled about in the kilt and sang sentimental songs about the bens and glens. But even his imitators did not look or sound very like him.

We are a nation of individuals and, though we may adopt models, we remain individuals and end up doing our own thing. That has been true of our Scottish—or, as they are properly called, like Scotch whisky, Scotch shortbread, Scotch porridge and Scotch broth—*Scotch* comedians. None of them has ever really resembled Lauder, and all of them have been very different from one another.

As for the kilt, it has not been prominent in the make-up of the comedians I shall be dealing with in this book. It is true that Lauder, who was a very deliberate artist and always knew what he was doing,

11

established the kilt as part of the uniform of the Scottish entertainer, and not only the comedian.

We have a Lowland word for the Highlander, which is often used in this connection in our entertainment world—"Teuchter." A show which displays the tartan is known in the business as a "Teuchter show." The kind of band which is used to accompany country dance—something like what the Irish might call a "ceilidh band," and which would be likely to make great use of the accordion and perhaps the fiddle, and use the kilt as working clothes—is called a "Teuchter band." And a typical Scottish touring show has this stamp about it. Andy Stewart's and Alec Finlay's TV shows are of this variety.

But the kilt is not employed to any great extent nowadays as a prop for comedy. It is more likely to be worn for Scots song and dance.

Even Harry Lauder did not always appear in the kilt. For many of his comedy numbers he wore trousers, the shabby dress of "the saftest o' the family" or the sailor suit of "We parted on the shore." Many of Lauder's performances were character acts. The portrayal of comic Scottish character, more Lowland than Highland, has been a strong line with many of his predecessors, contemporaries and successors.

Lauder, born in Portobello when that seaside village near Edinburgh was a place where a vigorous Lowland Scots was spoken, used dialect in his act, and dialect is still a useful commodity with almost all Scotch comedians. Yet even the use of Scots words is not indispensable to our laughter-raisers.

That erudite Yorkshire comedian, Stainless Stephen, who made many trips north of the Border in the Moss' Empire circuit, used to contend to me that our Scotch comics only required to show their tartan underpants and say "Och ay!" in order to set the gallery and the pit in a roar. He worked hard on his epigrammatic scripts and might be excused for some sourness at the apparent ease with which some of our entertainers, by sheer clowning and by local references and almost meaningless phrases which immediately put them into communication with their audience, could evoke belly laughs such as quips worthy of Oscar Wilde or Bernard Shaw could never achieve. But he over-simplified the ingredients of Scotch comedy.

He also overlooked its variety, and the many streams and tributaries which fed it. In contrast to the character comedians who had some affinity to one side of Lauder's talent—Neil Kenyon and Will Fyffe, for instance—there was a whole line of comedians who derived much more from the French mimes of the Jean Gaspard Deburau tradition, the

12

Italian-English clowns (Grimaldis, Bolenos, Lupinos) who were featured in the British pantomime, and the elaborately made-up Augustes and Joeys of the circus ring, than from the kilt and the wiggly walking stick or from the long tradition of character comedy. Such men were George West, Tommy Lorne, Bert Denver and Jack Anthony, who used clowns' make-up—"on with the motley, the paint and the powder"—and introduced a great deal of physical clowning into their acts.

Our physical clown *par excellence* was Dave Willis. He was greatly influenced by Charlie Chaplin and by the Lupinos. And yet Willis was quite distinct from Chaplin and never attained the acrobatic skill of the Italian-English race of clowns. In addition to some of Chaplin's miming he employed the comic effect of the familiar Scottish (Lowland working-class) phrase, and the child-like comic song, reminiscent of the "stotting rhymes" used by children when bouncing balls in the street.

Chaplin was such a master of mime that he was understandably reluctant to introduce speech even when the all-talking, all-singing sound films had ousted the good old silent movie which he had made his own, and in which he was understood all round the world. When he did decide to open his mouth on film, in *Modern Times*, it was in a *Finnegan's Wake* or Professor Stanley Unwin gibberish which could well be as universal as his miming. When he spoke at length, in *The Great Dictator*, it was not in the Cockney dialect which was native to him, and which he could have used for amusing effect, but in a King's English which would be understood in many lands.

Willis, on the other hand, like the average Scotch comedian, was content to be local in his humour, but with his element of physical clowning he still appealed to visitors who would miss the significance of his Scots phrases. "The clown," Chaplin has said, "is a figure in the dance," and that was Willis.

What he managed to take over of Chaplin's universality may have had a great deal to do with the fact that his Howard and Wyndham summer shows established records for their long runs. He was one successor to Lauder who could speak Scots, and yet be understood by the English and the Americans.

Almost all our Scotch comedians have had their origin in the industrial working class, and it is largely to that class that they have had their appeal, though their comedy has been an ideal escape also for the middle class and the tired business man. The middle class takes a delight in "going slumming," and watching the stage capers of men in bonnets and mufflers —the Tommy Morgans and Lex McLeans—and in listening to jokes

13

in broad Scots or Glasgow slang. Incongruity is the source of the belly laugh, and there is nothing more incongruous to us Scots than hearing a word of our old vernacular spoken in the wrong situation, or, conversely, a person addicted to Lowland speech trying to talk posh, or, as we say, "high-pan" or "pan-loaf."

Rikki Fulton and Jack Milroy, who achieved comic fame in a Scots double act, far removed from the tartan—in fact, caricaturing the dress, haircuts and manners of the Teddy Boy—derive part of their humour from this dichotomy of speech which afflicts working-class and lower middle-class Scots. Many of us have had experience of being scolded for using Scots words instead of English, both in the family circle and at school.

Scots in our time had become the language of the street, the playground and the factory floor. To talk it in the classroom, the drawing room, and even in the working-class kitchen when visitors were being entertained, was a social lapse. In the classroom, when a boy used Scots in answer to a teacherbe cause he could not think of the appropriate English word, it always raised a laugh among his classmates, and the same effect is obtained with a Scottish audience by the use of Scots words—and urban slang—on the stage.

Jack Milroy talks a rapid and racy Scots that is sometimes difficult even for Scots to follow, but sounds funny in any case; while Rikki Fulton excels in the caricature of the working-class Scottish youth trying to talk high-falutin' English. Rikki's jawbreakers are characteristic of certain types of Scots, who find it easier to acquire an impressive English vocabulary than to master the grammar, the idiom or the pronunciation of what was, until the seventeenth century, a foreign tongue to the people of Scotland. This malapropism was always a feature also of Irish and of Cockney humour.

The comic effect of racy Scottish speech goes quite far back in our traditions. When the Scots were trying hard to learn English—for the Common Market which we entered with the Treaty of Union in 1707—even the members of Parliament who took lessons in southern diction, from the Irishman Sheridan, caused laughter in the House of Commons whenever they opened their mouths. As the clown compensates for being an object of ridicule by acting the fool deliberately, we Scots soon learned that we could gratify the Englishman's sense of superiority by uttering our Scotticisms. The English laugh at all foreigners, and at the Scots no less.

Lauder discovered that the English could not distinguish between broad Scots, and good English spoken with a slight Scottish accent. So he was able to sound Scottish without being so cryptic that his English audiences lost the point of his jokes. This is a lesson our Scots comics have to learn when their audience is largely non-Scottish, and many of our Scotch comedians—Will Fyffe and Stanley Baxter spring to mind—have been able to adapt themselves when they moved south.

On TV, in *Dad's Army*, John Laurie can sound Scotch without uttering a single word of the language. Jimmy Logan achieves the same effect on the London West End stage by talking clear English in his natural accent. Sir James Barrie and James Bridie showed the way also in their plays, and the American musical *Brigadoon* achieved a Scottish sound with the employment of only two or three words of Scots.

But even when Scots was spoken by the Court as well as by the working people, laughter could be raised in Scotland by the use of outlandish words and reference to the outlandish manners of the "wilder Scots." A poet in the vernacular, of the calibre of Robert Fergusson of Edinburgh, could create amusement by quoting the quite different dialect of "the Buchan bodies on the beach," and the Highland Town Guard, with their broken English, and exaggerations of their Gaelic forms of speech. Sir Walter Scott employed distinctive dialect touches and Gaelicisms for a laugh, even though he spoke broad Scots himself.

Indeed the roots of our Scotch theatrical comedy go back much farther in our national history. They go back at least as far as the Middle Ages. The summer fairs and Beltane festivals, with their miming and mumming, and their dressing up of men in women's clothes, and the Yuletide minstrelsy and visitations of guisers, are recaptured today, not only in the Common Ridings and Beltane galas and parades, and the Halloween and Hogmanay guisers and "goloshans" of childhood, but also in the seaside and city summer shows and the Christmas and New Year pantomimes which retain their popularity in Scottish towns. "Drag" did not start with Danny La Rue. Our pantomime dames go back to the Maid Marians of the Robin Hood plays which were sometimes officially encouraged, sometimes condemned, banned and even punished by kirk and State, because they had a habit of becoming too popular and getting out of hand. Even the pantomime horse has its ancestor in the hobby horse of the clowns who accompanied the Morris dancers.

Although the drama, including comedy, had a difficult time at almost every stage in Scotland's history, and not simply at the hands of the Calvinists, there is some evidence that in the Middle Ages Scotland was more advanced than England in the quality of its theatrical performances.

The excellence of the Elizabethans in London altered the balance completely, and Scotland has not to this day caught up with England in the matter of drama.

William Dunbar's fragment, *Ane Littil Interlud of the Droichis* (Dwarf's) *Part of the Play*, is the only example we have left, in manuscript or in print, of the early Scottish drama or comedy. The dwarf in this court entertainment uses the skill of the clown in turning the edge of the sadistic laughter of larger people. He pretends to believe that he is a giant and claims to be descended from Finn McCool, Gow MacMorn, Gog Magog and other gigantic characters whom he describes with sometimes obscene relish.

Old Scots humour can be quite coarse. It smells of the refuse heaps which stood quite near to medieval homes, even to palaces, and it is fond of what we would now call lavatory or chamber-pot humour. You will find these elements in the poems on fairs, *Christ's Kirk on the Green* and *Peebles to the Play*, which are believed to have been composed by courtly writers, even by kings, and which laugh at the predicaments of common people, and at characters landing in the mire.

Laughter at little people in particular is an old Scottish tradition. They did not need to be dwarfs. Many of our Scottish comedians, particularly supporting comics, and stooges, have been wee men.

Little Dando in W. F. Frame's travelling show was a dwarf, and Harry Niblock, the foil to the tall and skinny Tommy Lorne, was diminutive. Alec Finlay is short of stature. So were Lauder, Willis and Harry Gordon. So now is one of Edinburgh's exports to London—Ronnie Corbett.

An interesting study might be made of the physical characteristics which predispose people to become comics, amateur or professional. Small people, awkwardly tall or skinny people, fatties, bespectacled types, redheads and people with unusual voices or accents are liable to become the butts of unfeeling ridicule, and they may protect themselves by beating their critics to the laugh.

A fat woman in a bathing costume screams to draw attention to herself, as if thinking: "They are going to look and laugh at me in any case: I might as well start the ball rolling." It is like the action of the employee who says: "You can't sack me: I'm leaving."

The inevitable target of sadistic fun says, in effect: "You can laugh if you like: I started it." This psychological syndrome probably explains why we Scots, like our Jewish friends, tell jokes against ourselves. Self-satire is a subtle form of self-defence, a kind of psychological judo.

16

The first of the few Scotch comedians to make an impact on world theatre, Sir Harry Lauder broke records on Broadway, toured everywhere and became a legend in his time, and for many people abroad the image of the Scot.

Will Fyffe, the greatest of the Scotch character comedians, was the son of a barn-stormer or strolling player and learned the art of entertainment in the travelling theatre.

Scots have been credited with being the tallest race in Europe, but we have a lot of wee folk among us. They seem to abound in the densely populated industrial areas, and particularly in the West of Scotland.

Anthropologists have suggested that there were tall Celtic people and small dark Celtiberian types, related to the Berbers of North Africa or the Portuguese, Mediterranean at any rate, among the indigenous population of Scotland. The cramped conditions of the crowded cities, especially Glasgow, may have favoured the survival of the wee men, who have been called troglodytes, *Fir Bolg* and other names.

Glasgow comics refer to "a shachlie wee bachle." *Shachlie* means knockneed and shuffling, and *bachle* or *bauchle* means a dilapidated old shoe, or a person in a similar state of decrepitude.

The juxtaposition of tall and short people, "the long and short of it," is classical in comedy—Morecambe and Wise, Revnell and West, Tommy Lorne and Harry Niblock, Lex McLean and Jimmy Carr, Weary Willie and Tired Tim, Don Quixote and Sancho Panza. On TV, Lex McLean has another Carr, Walter, as his foil, and he is not small like Jimmy, but taller than the principal comic; nevertheless, a contrast is maintained, with the positions reversed.

Mutt and Jeff were probably the most famous of the long and short partnerships in the strip cartoon world, which often employs similar devices to those of the variety stage. The *Daily Record* used to run a cartoon in which a dumpy Sir Harry Lauder was paired with a tall and skinny-legged Tommy Lorne, and it used the advertising slogan: "Laugh every morn with Lauder and Lorne." When Tommy died, Dave Willis and Harry Gordon were brought into the cartoon, but the classical contrast of the long and the short was lost. It was not quite so effective either when the twosome became a threesome.

To return to the roots of Scotch comedy, in the tortured history of the theatre in early Scotland, most of the records are lost, but here and there, through gaps in the mist, we glimpse evidence that at least a few people succeeded in putting on satiric comedies which gave the ordinary people a chance to laugh at the establishment. Around 1540, James Wedderburn produced plays which "nipped the abuses and superstitions of the time." His comedy, *The History of Dionysius the Tyrant*, was acted on the playing fields of Dundee. Social, political and even religious (anti-clerical) satire was a feature of the country's comedy, even in the days before the Reformation, when it must have been a risky exercise of liberty.

The fun and games, at the popular festivals—which were sometimes encouraged and sometimes repressed, causing riots—made a point of turning everything topsy-turvy. Men became women, beggars became kings, and there was an Abbot of Unreason—in Aberdeen he was called the Abbot of Bon Accord—who led the revels and encouraged the mob to turn the world "tapsilteerie."

Robin Hood was an anti-authoritarian figure and his girl, Maid Marian, was, like "Charley's Aunt," what would now be called a "drag artist," like the dames and Ugly Sisters of modern pantomime.

Innate in all the fun was criticism of the social set-up, and there were times when rulers thought it wise for the people to get their discontents out of their system in this way, and times when the fun turned as violent as a modern trainload of soccer fans.

The authorities, regal and ecclesiastic, must have worried considerably about the most popular pre-Reformation play in Scotland—Sir David Lyndsay's *Ane Pleasant Satyre of the Thrie Estates in Commendatioun of Vertew and Vituperation of Vyce*. The author was the Lyon King of Arms, the chief herald, the man responsible for scripting the national pageantry; so here was a member of the establishment subjecting the establishment to some very broad ridicule. In fact, it was performed before the king, and its criticism of the church actually led the monarch to call on the Bishop of Glasgow and his confreres to mend their ways.

Its earliest authenticated performance was before the king at Linlithgow on the Feast of the Epiphany, January 6, 1540, so it was a kind of Christmas pantomime. It may have been performed previous to that, at Cupar, Fife. It was certainly enacted at one time on Cupar Castle Hill. In 1554 the Queen Regent saw it performed at Greenside, now part of Edinburgh, near the spot where the Theatre Royal stood until burned down at the end of the war and the new St James's Development has arisen. The Playhouse cinema dominates Greenside today.

Revivals of *The Thrie Estaitis* at Edinburgh Festivals have shown the talent of Scots players in a great range of dramatic expression, from noble acting to robust clowning. In its modern text by Robert Kemp, with music by Cedric Thorpe Davie and directed by Tyrone Guthrie, it figured in the careers of two of our best-known Scotch comics—Duncan Macrae and Stanley Baxter. In 1973 we looked forward to another revival at the Festival, directed and re-scripted by Bill Bryden, with Rikki Fulton in the part of "Flatterie," later disguised as a pardoner, which was made famous by Macrae. "Flatterie" is a great part for a talented comedian. The script is broad and calls for wholehearted drollery.

20

Macrae played the pardoner selling relics and indulgences as if he were a cheapjack at a cattle market selling a trayful of trash:

"Here is ane relic, lang and braid,
Of Finn MacCool the richt chaft blade
  With teeth and all together:
Of Colin's cow, here is ane horn,
For eating of MacConnel's corn,
  Was slain into Balquidder.
Here is ane cord, baith great and lang,
That hangit John the Armstrang,
  Of guid hemp, soft and sound:
Guid, halie people, I stand for'd,
Wha ever beis hangit with this cord
  Needs never to be drouned."

The script is subtle and clever, but leaves ample room for physical buffoonery. Sir David Lyndsay, like the vaudeville artistes of our generation, knew well that a bishop falling on his backside would get a quicker laugh than a well-turned satiric line.

After the Reformation the kirk felt uncomfortable about plays which were not based on the Bible, and claimed the right to censor them, suppressing almost all "profane" productions. King James was fond of the theatre, however, and in 1599 he forced the clergy to rescind an act that "nane resort to these profane comedies for eschewing offence of God," based on a previous enactment passed against slanderous and indecent comedies. At King James's behest the Privy Council proclaimed that citizens of Edinburgh should be permitted to attend certain performances without incurring "ony pane, skaith, censuring, reproche or sclander."

If Calvinism had already set in, with its blighting influence on the Scottish stage, there is no sign of it in *Ane verie excellent and delectable Treatise entitled Philotus*. It was published in 1603 at Edinburgh, where it was publicly performed, and it purported to show "the greit inconvenience that fallis out in the Marriage between Age and Youth." Jack Ronder has written a modern version of *Philotus*. In its 1603 form (the year was that of the Union of Crowns), it is exceedingly permissive, and indulges in "drag artistry" carried to the limits of coarseness.

2

And in came Panto

THERE was not much indulgence for the theatre in Scotland thereafter. Eventually short plays, interludes and farces were inserted into concerts. Allan Ramsay's attempt to establish a theatre in Edinburgh was short-lived, but his cantata, *The Gentle Shepherd*, with its Scottish pastoral setting and its element of humour, achieved a long-lasting popularity. In a Festival revival of this also, Duncan Macrae had an opportunity to display his talent for clowning.

Robert Fergusson and Robert Burns shared Ramsay's ambition to write for the theatre, and both succeeded in writing scripts for delivery by famous players of the time. Burns's *Jolly Beggars* showed that he could have scripted a good piece of theatrical drollery, and both this and his *Tam o' Shanter* were dramatised as openings to the pantomimes in Scotland last century. But the real reawakening of Scottish theatre came with the dramatisation, what Sir Walter Scott gratefully called the "Terryification," of some of the *Waverley Novels*, the most popular last century, and up to the thirties of this century, being *Rob Roy*. The original performance of Charles Mackay in the part of Bailie Nicol Jarvie was the start of modern Scotch comedy acting.

Rob Roy (revived a few years ago for the State visit of King Olaf) was first put on by command of King George IV on August 27, 1822, in the course of his State visit to Edinburgh. His choice of the play was intended as a compliment to Scotland and to Sir Walter Scott, whom he liked personally. Edmund Kean, the famous actor, was then appearing in Edinburgh and had expected the King to "wish" to see him playing *Macbeth*. The King's choice of the Scott play offended Kean, and left him under the impression that he was disliked at Court.

However, it was a great night for Edinburgh, and for the Theatre Royal in Shakespeare Square at the foot of the Bridges, a theatre built at a cost of £5,000 and opened on December 9, 1769, to seat a £140 audience.

This theatre, by the way, lasted until 1859, and among its stars was Mr Wyndham, who first appeared in the Shakespeare Square theatre in 1845 after making his reputation in the Theatre Royal, Glasgow. Later he opened a new Theatre Royal at the Adelphi in Edinburgh, the one near Greenside. This was the start of the Howard and Wyndham theatrical enterprises, which have meant a great deal to the fortunes of the Scotch comics whom we are considering.

Scott's sponsoring of *Rob Roy* was a great help to the Shakespeare Square theatre, and to Mrs Henry Siddons, whose business as lessee was in a bad way financially at the time. *Rob Roy* had been seen in an earlier dramatised version at the Pantheon, Broughton Street (the future Adelphi and Theatre Royal), on January 17, 1818. Then came a musical version, *Rob Roy MacGregor, or Auld Lang Syne*, presented with great success in Covent Garden, London, and running for forty-one consecutive nights at the Shakespeare Square theatre, starting on February 15, 1819. Its Rob Roy was Mr Hamerton, with Mrs Renaud as Helen MacGregor, Mr Duff as Dougal Cratur, and Charles Mackay as Bailie Nicol Jarvie. Scott fell rapturously in love with Mackay's characterisation of the Bailie and wrote to the actor in the most enthusiastic terms about it, over the signature "Jedediah Cleishbotham."

In 1821, the year before King George's Scottish visit, Charles Mackay was called to Covent Garden for a one-night stand as the Bailie. Sir Walter wrote to Lord Montague: "There is a young man going up from Edinburgh to play one night at Covent Garden, whom, as having the very unusual power of presenting on the stage a complete Scotsman, I am very anxious you should see. He plays Bailie Nicol Jarvie in *Rob Roy*, but with a degree of national truth and understanding which makes the part equal to anything I have ever seen on the stage, and I have seen all the best comedians these forty years. . . . The English will not enjoy it,

23

for it is not broad enough nor sufficiently caricatured for their apprehensions; but to a Scotsman, it is inimitable, and you have the Glasgow Bailie before you, with all his bustling conceit and importance, his real benevolence and his irritable habits."

Mackay made such a hit in London that his one-night stand ran to six nights. He performed other Scottish comedy characters, including Dominie Sampson from *Guy Mannering* and the Laird of Dumbiedykes from *The Heart of Midlothian*, which had been dramatised as *Jeanie Deans, or The Lily of St Leonards*.

Sir Walter Scott was a noisy and demonstrative theatregoer. When he first sat in a box with his family to see Mackay as the Bailie, his laughter, at a character he had himself originally created, rang round the auditorium. In 1822 his vociferous enthusiasm for Mackay was to be shared with King George.

The command performance packed the theatre. The crowds for the pit and galleries gathered early in the day and were drenched in a rainstorm before the doors opened at 6 p.m. As soon as the doors were thrown open, the audience rushed in savagely, and after the "House Full" notice had gone up, many people were still crashing their way in.

In the better seats there was a resplendent array of well-dressed citizens, including a brave display of tartans and uniforms. The audience sang Scottish songs to pass the time until the occupants of the boxes arrived about 7.30 p.m. His Majesty was received at the door by the Duke of Montrose and Mr Murray, manager of the theatre, carrying silver candlesticks.

The King wore the uniform of a marshal. He took his seat in a royal box, in which something like a throne had been prepared for him. With him were the Dukes of Montrose and Argyll, the Marquis of Winchester, the Earl of Fife, Lord Cathcart, Lord Groves and Lord Glenlyon.

The National Anthem was sung at King George's arrival and again at the end of the performance, when a verse was added which greatly affected the monarch. It referred to the death of George III.

> "Bright beams are soon o'ercast,
> Soon our brief hour is past,
>   Losing our King.
> Honour'd, beloved and dear,
>
> Still shall his parting ear
> Our latest accents accents hear:
>   God save the King!"

Although there were already old-timers saying there would never be another Rob Roy like Mr Hamerton, the star of the 1819 production, the Rob Roy of the royal occasion was Mr Calcraft, a Newcastle man, and former cavalry officer, who had acted with Edmund Kean, and who later became a theatre manager in Dublin. The villainous Rashleigh Osbaldistone was played by Mr Denham, Francis by Mr Huckel, Helen MacGregor once more by Mrs Renaud and Dougal by Mr Duff. Diana Vernon, for one night only, was none other than Mrs Henry Siddons.

The show was presented "with the original music and appropriate scenery, machinery, dresses and decorations." There were the great scenic effects which survived into our times—the Old Bridge of Glasgow, the College Gardens and View of the Spire of St Mungo, the Clachan of Aberfoyle and Distant View of the Highland Loch, the Pass of Lochard, a Romantic Glen in the Highlands and View of Loch Lomond, Moonlight.

But most of all it was Mackay's Bailie that the King relished. His Majesty laughed out loud at the magistrate's laying about him with a "het poker" in self-defence, and the remark: "Nane o' your London tricks here!" His fat sides heaved at the Bailie's commendation of the wee Highland laddie: "That's a braw callant! Ye'll be a man before your mither yet."

The King enjoyed Mr Huckel's singing of "My love is like a red, red rose," but thought another song was off-beat and tried to correct it with a wave of his hand. His favourite song was "I'll gang nae mair to yon toun."

On leaving, he told Mr Murray how pleased he was to see his old favourite, Mrs Henry Siddons, again; and he left a substantial donation to the funds of the needy theatre. In his carriage on the way home to Dalkeith Palace he was still laughing at Mackay's cantrips and sallies, and he expressed the opinion that the play was neither too short nor too long, but entirely delightful.

These dramatised *Waverley Novels* were the great draw for the Scottish masses for over a hundred years. Sometimes the two theatres in Glasgow would stage rival *Rob Roys* simultaneously, giving the critics a fine chance to compare the casting and the performances. While Mackay was still on the boards, some of his rivals in the part of the Bailie were criticised for playing down to the audience, especially by introducing anachronistic Glasgow slang into the part.

There was a Mr McGregor, who infuriated one critic by introducing the comic remark: "I'll gie ye a slap on the muns." The worn *muns* does not occur even in *Parliamo Glasgow* (Stanley Baxter's name for the

25

city's mixture of dialect and slang) or, as it has sometimes been called, *Glescaranto* (on the analogy of *Esperanto*). Rhyming slang has always been a favourite with the Glaswegians as with the Cockneys, and *muns* had its origin in the shyming slang of Pierce Egan and other reporters of the old Prize Ring, who referred to the eyes as *the mince* (from *mince pies*, rhyming slang for *eyes*).

"Mr McGregor, as the 'Bailie'," wrote the stern Glasgow critic, "takes liberties with the text, which would have made the hair of Sir Walter Scott stand on end. . . . It is not necessary, in representing a Scotchman, to make him vulgar, and, as a brother Scot, he ought not, by misrepresentation, to bring his countrymen into disrepute . . . The Bailie was a respectable citizen, who was shocked at the Highlanders whistling on a Sunday, and who only gave utterance to an oath, when under great excitement.

"Mr McGregor presents him as a denizen of the Saltmarket of the present day, and not of the time when it was the seat of commerce, and the most fashionable street of the city; and many of his quaint old forms of speech are lost in the low phrases of modern date. . . . With such an audience the greatest care ought to be taken, and the text rather purified than alloyed—instead of each sentence being garnished with an oath, the few in the text would be well omitted."

This was obviously a voice crying in the wilderness, for Mr McGregor and his contemporary comedians were playing for quicker and louder laughs than would have contented either Sir Walter Scott or Charles Mackay. They were hitting their audience hard.

As Lex McLean once said to me in the dressing room of the now defunct Leith Gaiety: "Ye've got to hit them with the pail to make them forget all their problems."

Even in performances of *The Gentle Shepherd* and of *Cramond Bridge, or The Gudeman of Ballengeich*, the comics introduced their own gags to suit their audiences.

What made Glaswegians laugh over a hundred years ago is suggested in a critique of pantomime in this same fortnightly *Glasgow Dramatic Review* in 1845: "The grand feature in pantomime is the Clown, on him its success mainly depends: between Mr Hemmings and Mr Mason Boleno no point of comparison can possibly exist; the one is the very pink of stupidity, the other the very *acme* of drollery: they have nothing in common save the name, and we question Mr Hemming's title to that; he has nothing beyond a large mouth, an enormous tongue, which he continually lolls out, and a most stupid expression of face, with which to excite laughter. With such a stock in trade, no wonder he fails; he is in fact only fit to chalk a rope and tumble in the sawdust of a circus. But who can look on Masson Boleno and not laugh? From the time he utters 'Here we are' till the curtain falls, he keeps the audience in continual roars, makes them hold their aching sides and shout in very merriment; his look of astonishment, when Harlequin gives him a whack, is fun itself, and then his wink—oh, what a roguish wink!—drawing up the one side of his mouth till it claims brotherhood with his eye—is so irresistibly comic that we defy the most serious to resist it."

The harlequinade and the transformation scenes tended to disappear from panto in this century, but the importance of the comic increased—Buttons and the Uglies in *Cinderella*, Widow Twankey and Wishee-Washee in *Aladdin*, Idle Jack, Simple Simon and all the magnificent Bad Barons and Dames. In addition to the pantos at Christmas last century, there were the summer fairs to give the comics opportunities to develop their talents in the penny gaffs and circuses. Glasgow Fair at the foot of the Saltmarket, on the border of the green opposite the Court House, was going strong in the middle of last century, and native comedians had opportunities of studying the antics of the comic men in melodrama and the Italian-English clown families, the acrobatic drolls such as the Bolenos and Lupinos, who demonstrated the use of mime and knock-about humour.

Often the two strains of comedy—exaggerated character acting and sheer buffoonery—have become mixed. By the time music-hall, vaudeville or variety had arrived in Scotland, even the characters in the dramatised *Waverley Novels* had acquired more than a touch of pantomime. The Dougal Cratur was winning laughs with "See the muckle white craw!" (addressed to the English captain to distract his attention from the Highlander's hiding the bribe money in his stocking) and "The wee man's gotten his parritch at last" when Rashleigh, the villain, was dispatched. Andrew Fairservice, the gardener, who in Scott's novel is a worthy old Scot and the vehicle for some of the author's best observations in the vernacular, had become a front-cloth stand-up comic, keeping the audience amused with Glasgow humour, some of it quite anachronistic and all of it broad, while the scene-shifters got busy behind the drop scene with the setting of the next big effect.

By the thirties of this century, when *Rob Roy* still had a following as a summer show, Fairservice was in the trews and tammy of a music-hall comic, with a whip in one hand and a gigantic scone, with a large bite out of it, in the other. Sometimes he even sprayed crumbs as he talked, a quick-fire method of getting a laugh. He had degenerated into the comic man of the Victorian melodrama.

27

Kailyard drama had its offspring in the couthy music-hall sketches, such as *The Concealed Bed* and *The Wash-House Key*, which presented the humours of Scottish working-class life. Variety audiences were not in the mood for subtle characterisation. They liked broad comedy alternating with strong sentiment.

When Joe Corrie, the Fife miner poet and playwright, put his one-acters on, in the Depression of the twenties and thirties, with a team of unemployed people from the coalfield, he found it easier to obtain laughs than to awaken his audience to the social implications. When he turned on the sentiment, it had to be signalled to the audience with slow music by the theatre orchestra: otherwise it would be killed in the hilarity which his Fife expressions and the cantrips of his comics had aroused. Many of his audience were as hard hit by the Depression as his players and himself: while they were pleased to know that someone was concerned about social inequalities, they still welcomed a good laugh.

3

The Waggle o' the Kilt

I STOOD in the wings of the Alhambra Theatre, Glasgow. Beside me was G. H. Elliot, the Chocolate-Coloured Coon, with his brown make-up rubbed off, and garbed in his dressing gown. He was gazing intently at the centre of the stage, saying: "What an artist!"

It was war-time, and the man who occupied the centre of the stage was Sir Harry Lauder, an old star performing for charity. He was flanked by two other famous Scotch comedians—Dave Willis and Harry Gordon. I had written a song for them, a song which they never sang, though it was later featured by Miff Smith and Henry Hall's Band—"Don't believe the rumours that you hear."

Both Willis and Gordon had been enthusiastic about the song and had learned and rehearsed it, but at the last minute Lauder (although I had given him all the pay-off lines) decided: "We won't sing it. I have a better song than that." No one required to be told what his choice of song was: at that time he was singing nothing else but "Keep right on to the end of the road." And that was the one it had to be, with Willis and Gordon and eventually the whole audience, and everyone on stage, joining in the chorus.

G. H. Elliot was quite a music-hall artist himself, and one who studied every step, gesture, position and modulation of voice in his song-and-dance act. He was seeing once more, and possibly for the last time, how Lauder held the stage, the swing of his broad shoulders and short legs in Highland dress, the gestures, the eyes; and listening to that still strong baritone which vibrated clearly to the highest seat in the gods.

Not long before that, I had seen Lauder, in a Rutherglen cinema, imperiously order the manager to remove the microphone from the stage, as if it were an abomination, and an insult to his art. He belonged to a generation which learned to keep its chin elevated to the upper circle and which could make a whisper carry to the topmost row in the gallery.

Lauder may not have been our funniest comedian or our greatest vocalist. There were many things in the repertoire of other entertainers at which he made no attempt. But he was undoubtedly meticulous in the way he thought out and planned his act, to the smallest detail. To watch him rehearse the orchestra was a revelation.

His authoritarian command of the stage, and of everyone involved in his act, developed in him the pomposity of a conductor. Offstage, he carried himself with the air, not of a comic, or even of a star, but of a prominent public figure, on the level of a Prime Minister at least, and not far removed from Royalty. In fact, at the opening of the Empire Exhibition (Scotland) 1938, there was a red carpet laid right across the field of the White City for the Royal party to walk upon, and, until they arrived, no one would walk on it: except Lauder, who acted as if it had been put down especially for him.

There was a stage in his career when this self-importance endangered his act. I once heard him get the bird from a working-class audience in Edinburgh. It was when he had come to think of himself as a leader of thought on the problems of the day—particularly industrial unrest.

His curtain lectures had been accepted in the course of the Great War, when they were appeals to help the soldiers and sailors and their families, or the fishermen in the minesweepers. But when, in the twenties, he started to harangue striking miners, and to advise them, "speaking as an ex-miner," to go back to the pits, he was plainly asking for it.

Eventually he "came off it," but I doubt if he ever saw anything wrong in what he had been doing. He was not simply the comedian dying to play Hamlet: he was the comic who thought he could preach—a delusion which can be fatal.

But there is no question about the greatness of Lauder in his own sphere. The man who took the London music halls by storm and made hard-bitten Yankee showmen gasp with amazement at his success on Broadway was surely, like King James VI and I, "the wisest fool in Christendom."

He was born in a but and ben, a humble cottage, in Bridge Street, just off Main Street, Portobello, and he carried the accents of that broad-spoken Edinburgh suburb round the world, fortified by the accents of Angus and Lanarkshire.

His MacLennan blood entitled him to wear the kilt and it became hi identification as a Scotsman as well as his chief property as a comedian. He established the kilt as the prescribed wear for Scottish entertainers, particularly singers and comics; and many still wear it off-stage, as he did.

He was proud of having risen from the working class and of having had his schooling as a half-timer in Arbroath while earning his living as a boy in a flax-spinning mill. He made much of the fact that he had been a miner, though no doubt he was even more satisfied that he had early made his escape from the pits. His rise, from going on with a song at concerts in Arbroath, to success on the stage, was rapid.

He wrote most of his songs, some of which have become so well established nationally that there is confusion whether he composed them, or Robert Burns. He even wrote a Scottish comedy.

He was a star long before the Great War of 1914-18, and had several "farewell world tours" between the wars. He survived the Second World War, dying on February 26, 1950, at the age of 79, a national figure. The story of his life, and of his remarkable stage career, has been well told, not only by Lauder himself in *Harry Lauder at Home and on Tour*, *A Minstrel in France*, *Roamin' in the Gloamin'* and other books, but also recently by Gordon Irving. I shall deal rather with my own impressions and recollections, and the anecdotes of Lauder I have collected from time to time from meeting people who knew him well.

In Longstone, on the outskirts of Edinburgh, in 1959, I spoke to a retired gamekeeper, George Ross, who had looked after Lauder when Sir Harry was fishing the Tummel (golf, shooting, motoring and salmon fishing were the comedian's hobbies, and he loved exploring his ancestral Highlands, so different from the industrial Lowlands in which he had been reared).

George Ross thought Lauder was a wonderful man, a great character and, what a gamekeeper most appreciated, very keen on the fishing. When they were sitting waiting on an elusive fish to return, Lauder told him a story of a time when he was going north to Aberdeen with his concert party, and left them at Perth, at an unearthly hour, to visit some friends he had promised to call on at Luncarty. He found his friends' house deserted, so returned to Luncarty station to wait for the train.

There was a sonsy farmer sitting at the station. Sir Harry spoke to him and got no reply.

Lauder said to himself: "I'll get something out of this man before I'm done." While the farmer was reading his paper, Sir Harry asked the porter: "What do you call this station?" The porter said: "Luncarty South." Sir Harry asked him again, and again a third time, until the porter was at the end of his patience.

When the train came in, Sir Harry followed the farmer into a carriage, and commented to him: "I have travelled the world, and I have never been insulted as I've been at this station." The farmer said, "If you were insulted here, it must have been your own fault."

Sir Harry replied, "I'll bet you if you ask the porter the name of the station you'll get dog's abuse. I'll bet you five to one." And to prove his point he pulled down the window and shouted to the porter: "What station is this?"

The porter flew into a rage and answered: "To hell with you and the station!" and Sir Harry remarked to the farmer: "What did I tell you?"

This story illustrates Lauder's irrepressible strain of mischievous humour and practical jokes, and how he relished recounting such incidents afterwards. I had another story about him from his close friend, Mr John Quigley, secretary of the Cowal Highland Games. He was with Lauder on a visit to Carlisle, and they walked to the train, on an afternoon so hot that the comedian grew thirsty, bought a small bottle of beer from the buffet and sipped it on the way to his carriage. A porter followed with Lauder's luggage, and put it into the compartment.

Lauder got in with Mr Quigley, pulled down the window and leaned out of it, chatting to the porter, until the guard waved his flag for the train to depart. Said Lauder to the porter: "Do you take a drink?" Delighted, the porter, expecting a tip, replied: "Yes, sir." The comedian handed him the half-drunk bottle of beer as the train steamed out, leaving a bewildered porter looking after him with the bottle in his hand.

Sir Harry had placed another stone on the cairn of his remembrance as a mean Scotsman—a myth which he was pleased to perpetuate for publicity purposes, though he could be generous enough when he felt inclined. He used to say: "If folk think I'm mean, they'll no' expect too much."

It might be thought that the poor porter in Carlisle got nothing for his pains, but in fact he got a Lauder story he could tell for the rest of his life.

In a later chapter, I discuss the origins of the "mean Scot" joke and the way in which it was cultivated in the case of Sir Harry Lauder. Another story I heard on my wayfaring, in the North-East of Scotland this time, illustrates a peculiarity of Scottish humour, or an old attitude to it which might baffle a foreigner.

Sir Harry Lauder was up fishing on Deeside. He called for a cup of tea at a friend's house. The old lady of the family, seated at the head of the table, was weighing the comedian up rather suspiciously, but Sir Harry went out of his way to entertain her. He told her funny story after funny story. She sat and stared without the shadow of a smile. Sir Harry left rather downhearted, feeling that he had not made a very favourable impression.

He sailed across the ocean to America. Some time later, while walking in Broadway, he was stopped by a man who said: "Well, I never! Lauder! You do get around: one week I see you in Deeside and now I meet you in New York. Do you remember old Mrs Fraser whom you visited in Deeside?"

Ruefully, Sir Harry admitted he remembered her. "Man," said the other, "she thinks the world of you. She took me in and showed me the chair you sat in, and said, 'Harry Lauder, the great comedian fae Edinburgh, he sat in that chair for twa hours telling me story efter story, and for twa hours it was a' I could dae to keep fae laughing."

I have mentioned Lauder's meticulousness in the presentation of his act, the way he drilled the orchestra and the care with which he studied his own gestures and voice inflections. At the same time he could perform on the stage with apparent artlessness, and some of his humour was at once subtle and profound. For instance, when he came on as the country carpenter or joiner, with a length of board on his shoulder, and announced: "This is a shelf for Mrs Mackintosh's wee sweetie shop: I beat Sandilands for the contract."

It may have been caricature, but it was a deft comment on the relativity of values in a small country town, and one which even city audiences, often only a generation removed from the rural life, immediately appreciated. Then there was the realism of some of his acting—that cough he managed to simulate, a cough which he seemed to drag up from his boots, a cough prolonged until terminated on the very brink of overplaying, to be followed by the story that he had been to the doctor about it, and that the doctor had told him: "At your age, you should be glad of a cough like that."

This was Lauder's variant of a classical Highland story of two old men passing a graveyard. One remarked, "You've a bad cough, Donald," and the other replied, "Ach yes, but there's a lot of folk in there that would be glad of a cough like mine." Like almost all comedy material, Lauder's consisted of adaptations of traditional jokes.

In a radio request programme recently, I heard an old Lauder gramophone record played. It was "Will ye stop your tickling, Jock?" It reminded me of how we used to listen to Lauder away back before the Great War on the old-fashioned phonograph with the cylindrical record which announced itself as "Edison-Bell record . . . Harry Lauder singing." He must have been one of the earliest recorders with a wide popular appeal.

The recent replay illustrated his melodious singing and his infectious laughter. Long before radio, he had mastered the technique of communication, dependent on the voice alone, and his song and his laughter conveyed a picture of the man to millions who never saw him.

Even today, inured as we are to "laughing policemen" and such hilarious effects on disc and tape and on the air, it is impossible to listen to Lauder's "tickle-ickle-ickling" without a smile. Incidentally it shows also how the intimacies of courtship could be implied without colouring it blue. Lauder (and his generation of Scotch comedians took this leaf out of his book) stuck to clean humour on the stage, though he could relish a near-the-knuckle joke in masculine company, in private. If his "Stop your tickling" is regarded nowadays as corny, it is because public manners have changed radically even since his death in 1950, and vastly since he first trod the London music-hall boards at the beginning of the century.

Lauder's stage character—the little man in the kilt with the Balmoral, Kilmarnock or Tam o' Shanter bonnet, the long sporran, and the twisted walking-stick—was largely the product of Victorian sentimentalisation of the Highlander. The Georgians began it when, after banishing the Highland dress in punishment for the 1745 rising, they relented and, much under the romantic influence of Sir Walter Scott, had a great tartan revival associated with the visit of King George IV in 1822, at which not only the King but fat Sir William Curtis of London donned the kilt. Queen Victoria and Prince Albert encouraged the wearing of the kilt on their visits to Balmoral, and it was very much a Royal fashion when Lauder started his stage career at the end of last century.

Many think that Tommy Lorne was the greatest Scotch clown that ever capered on the stage. He was the darling of pantomime and revue patrons in the twenties and thirties.

Duncan Macrae, physically adapted to comic roles, was a straight actor who switched without difficulty to panto and revue, but returned to legitimate drama with equal facility.

He also appeared in many films and is here seen as Constable Maclean in Walt Disney's *Greyfriars Bobby*.

The Laird of Inversnecky, Harry Gordon, the Aberdeen seaside entertainer who failed to conquer London but had an enduring success in the big shows of Glasgow and Edinburgh.

Dave Willis, Chaplinesque with Scotch dressing, was the most visual and physical of our clowns, and broke records in city panto and summer show series.

It was also a great fashion among London cartoonists. When they wanted to represent a Scot, to illustrate a joke in *Punch* or a lampoon in some political periodical, they incorporated the Highland dress, and if Lauder wanted to be recognised as a Scot on the London music-halls, the kilt was the first essential, just as the stage Irishman was expected to wear a green tail-coat, knee-breeches, a Paddy hat with a clay pipe stuck in it, and brogues, while carrying a blackthorn stick. Indeed, when Lauder first trod the London boards, Irish comedians were more familiar to the Cockney public.

Lauder was the first to waggle the kilt, and his garb, his corkscrew stock, his cocky swagger and the little dance he performed at the bend, like a miniature Highland fling, all became part of his essential image in a music-hall world where all the leading performers had their hallmarks of dress and mannerism.

His attire and style at once tickled the Londoners and awoke nostalgia in the exiled Scots, of whom there were many in the English capital, and in the big centres of population which he visited abroad. Members of Caledonian societies in New York, Brisbane and other cities on his farewell world tours," helped to ensure him an enthusiastic audience. There were Scots who resented his "guying" of the kilt, but they did not represent the majority, who turned out to welcome him wherever he went, and who appreciated national subtleties in his act which the English, the Americans and the Australians probably missed.

Meanwhile he played up to the Englishman's, the American's and the Australian's conception of a Scot. His publicity snowballed as newspaper columnists latched on to his potentialities as a comic subject. In addition to the Lauder stories which he enacted or recounted, there arose a host of Lauder legends which were dreamed up by newspaper writers, especially in New York. The Scotch joke, with which I deal in a later chapter, was cultivated. Sometimes jokes of completely non-Scottish origin, which happened to fit the Lauder image, were adapted to the subject by American newspaper men.

As Lauder's stock rose abroad, naturally he gathered kudos at home, and after every triumphant tour he came back to Scotland to play the No. 1 dates in Edinburgh and Glasgow, and follow them up, by special request, by visits farther north. He would head the bill in a variety show, with the supporting items warming up the audience for his big entrance.

Now that we are accustomed to more modern techniques of presentation, it is difficult to recapture what a Lauder show really looked like in his heyday. Before revue and non-stop variety, and long before cinema musicals, and filmed, taped and edited TV variety, we were much more patient in waiting for the big act.

The orchestra played the Lauder melodies, swinging into the opening number as the curtains folded back to reveal a typically Scottish scene, then the wee kilted figure with the walking stick and the cheeky smile came prancing on to a crescendo of laughs and cheers. A wave of his expressive hand brought him silence for his song, which was broken by bursts of laughter at his quaint steps, facial expressions, and the jests in his verses. Then there was the pause for patter, in which he played the audience like a fish, with the orchestra coming in on cue for his closing chorus.

The music continued while he took several bows, and went on while he changed in the wings for his next number. The scene changed, and the melody, and back he came again in a change of costume, even if it was only a different colour of kilt.

He was very much a music-hall act, a "turn." He never really made the later media. He was filmed in *Huntingtower*, from the John Buchan novel, and other productions, but Lauder was no movie actor. It was left to Will Fyffe, his greatest successor, to become a hit on the talking screen, and to a much later generation of Scottish entertainers to make their name on TV. But in one other medium besides the variety stage he was, and has remained, great—the gramophone. He was on it from Edison-Bell phonograph days and sang in the earliest attempts at synchronised sound and cinema.

The kilted image was more necessary for Lauder abroad than at home. Here we know that in our urban and industrial surroundings the Highland dress is only occasional, if not a rarity. He created characters in other attire which fitted more into the modern scene—the sailor, the "Saftest o' the Family" and so on—but always the influence was distinctly kailyard. Even his non-kilted characters belonged to a Scotland that was vanishing, and that gave them, for nostalgic old Scots, part of their appeal.

His songs were distantly influenced by the love lyrics of Robert Burns and the strong Scottish folk song tradition, but from a severely critical point of view they were marred by the vulgar sentimentality of *Whistle Binkie*, a Victorian collection of verses which revealed the descent of our national verses from the melodic excellence of Burns and the magic of our great ballads. He had a talent for a simple, comic, sentimenta llyric and a catchy tune with the Scotch kick in it. The proof of the pudding is in the eating, and his lyrics and tunes caught on and have endured, however much the sterner pundits may deplore their incorporation into our "national heritage."

> "When the sun has gone to rest,
> That's the time that I love best—
> Oh, it's lovely roamin' in the gloamin'."

is obviously not great poetry of the quality of Burns's

> "The wan moon is setting behind the long wave
> And time is setting wi' me O!"

and

> "We parted on the shore and the ship began to roar"

is not in the same class as

> "The boat rows at the pier o' Leith . . . "

When Lauder began his concert singing in Scotland, the music-halls in Glasgow and Edinburgh drew a fair amount of their talent from the South. Sir Edward Moss and other variety managers kept their eyes on the London music-halls and invited successful artistes north, including Marie Lloyd. Occasional local talent had a chance to fill in.

Lauder's predecessors were usually in the Scottish character comedy tradition. J. C. Macdonald had a carter act in which the working attire and the whip of the carrier were meticulously copied, along with the mannerisms and expressions. It was very much in the style of Andrew Fairservice as that character had evolved in the later *Rob Roys*, or of Jock Howieson in *Cramond Brig*. It was vulgarised *Waverley Novels* characterisation for the entertainment of the music-hall masses. There was another comic singer, Curran, who specialised in parodies of well-known Scots songs. One of his remembered numbers was a parody of Scott's "Gather, gather, gather"—again from *Rob Roy*—in which Curran sang:

> "You may steal my land, you may steal my farm,
> But you can't steal the name that's tattooed on my arm."

J. M. Hamilton was another who represented local talent on the music-hall stage with Scottish songs and entertaining patter. W. F. Frame performed the comic Scot, including Scotch versions of the characters done by Dan Leno.

With Lauder's success beyond the bounds of Scotland, there was encouragement for others, and the word "Scotch comedian" became familiar on music-hall programmes alongside the singers and comedians from England on whom these programmes still mainly depended. Lauder's example of building a Scottish image on the wearing of the kilt was followed by Jock Mills and Donald McKay. Mills, like Lauder, obtained engagements in England and tours abroad, and retired to run a popular pub, Jock Mills' Bar, near Glasgow's Buchanan Street Station, which continued to be patronised by Scots and visitors who had never seen his act but accepted the fact that the proprietor was a Scotch comedian of the Lauder vintage.

A comedian very much in the Lauder tradition, featuring the kilt and Scottish songs and jokes, is Peter Sinclare, who has forged a career in England after working mostly in Glasgow about the beginning of the Second World War. Physically he is quite unlike Lauder, being built more like a Highland athlete, and darkly handsome, but he has kept alive a lot of the Lauder-type humour. He has played Scottish parts in musicals and has been probably best known as the kilted grandfather in the Jimmy Clitheroe comedies, in which he was a butt for the Lancashire comedian's sallies about the Scots. Sinclare has a good voice which has made him a natural radio artiste, a sphere in which Lauder was beginning to shine before his retirement.

Another comedian who used the kilt with comic effect was Ike Freeman, who combined the Scotch with the Jewish brand of humour as a "Hebrew Scot." He was a popular entertainer in the thirties, in summer shows and variety.

Two who have kept close to the Lauder tradition in tartan display and the singing of traditional and new Scottish songs are Alec Finlay and Andy Stewart, but both of these comedians require more extended treatment as important showmen in their own right, and will be dealt with in later chapters.

Jokes about the kilt formed part of the varied stock in trade of Ken Dodd recently on radio, using that versatile Scottish actor and comedian, John Laurie, as his butt. The joke goes right back to Scotland's own medieval poets—to William Dunbar in *The Flyting of Dunbar and Kennedy*, in which the Lowland makar ridicules the dress and speech of the Gaelic bard.

4

The Character Comedians

LAUDER was very much a solo act. On occasion, as in one presentation of *I Love a Lassie* which I remember, he would bring on a dancer or some other support, but for the most part he preferred to appear as the culmination of a series of variety acts and "fill the stage" by himself. As he did not use the microphone, he was entirely free to make the fullest use of the stage, and he sauntered around a lot as he sang and pattered.

I remember him in his seventies causing the audience to collapse in laughter with his opening sally: "I have just come from Strath Haven (using an exaggeratedly posh pronunciation of *Strathaven*, which is usually pronounced "Straiven")."

Neil Kenyon, who was an early contemporary of Lauder's, went in for feeds and supports, and indeed for well-scripted acts of the music-hall sketch type. More than Lauder, also, he presented modern urban types, or rural characters with only the slightest kailyard touches.

The music-hall sketch had become quite a feature of variety or vaudeville, and anticipated the tidy arrangement of revue and the modern non-stop variety show. A man who contributed greatly to the development of a distinctively Scottish music-hall sketch was Graham Moffat, born in 1866 in Glasgow. He died in Cape Town in 1951.

His father was a professor of elocution, and the family were almost all players. Graham Moffat wrote one of the few Scottish plays which have been resounding successes in London—*Bunty Pulls the Strings*, which has often been condemned as kailyard, but has always been undoubtedly funny and entertaining. Some of its comic characters continue to amuse, and have a family resemblance to the characters portrayed by our traditional comedians.

Moffat wrote innumerable scripts which are preserved in our libraries, but his most famous one, from the music-hall point of view, was *The Concealed Bed*, with which the Moffat family company toured from 1910 onwards. It was an uproarious farce about the predicament of people caught in one of these Victorian contraptions, and it was the talk of Scotland for many a year. The Moffats were active as players into the thirties, but there have been many revivals of *Bunty* and of *A Scrape o' the Pen*, including TV presentations, proving the appeal of this old-fashioned type of Scottish humour and sentiment even to the public of today.

Neil Kenyon, whom Lauder admired and encouraged, presented something which was not quite so elaborate as a music-hall sketch, but in which his songs and patter derived support from a set scene and the intervention of one or two feeds. Two scenes particularly remembered are a postman act in a village setting, and a shipboard act in a cabin. Kenyon's humour was dry. He would be front-stage addressing the audience with his confidences about the people of the village in which he was delivering the letters, when a character would come out from a house at the wings and cry: "Postie, have ye ony letters for me?" Neil would reply: "Only a postcaird, but I have-na read it yet."

In his ship scene, an engineer with a bald head and his cap under his arm would come in, and Neil would say: "Pit your cap on, man! You're half-naked." It was as simple—perhaps corny—stuff as that. But these phrases stick.

Like Sir Harry Lauder, Neil Kenyon was a diligent collector of stories with a distinctively Scottish flavour, and he worked them into his turns. For instance, as the postie, he told story after story about the characters to whom he was supposed to be delivering the letters. He would say: "Oh ay, this yin's for wee Jock up there at the Hillocks. He was a great lad for the silver-grey Dorkings and used to win prizes at the show wi' them. But the last time I saw him he said he had gien the chickens up and was rearing pigs instead. Says he to me, says he: 'The next time ye're up at the Hillocks I'll show ye the best litter in the country.'

"Weill, ye ken, the next time I was up there it was his wife that came to the door and I says til her, says I: 'Could I see the wee swine?'

" 'Oh,' says she, 'ye've juist missed him. He's awa doon the back road'."

Another of his stories was of meeting his pal Sandy in the village street, just outside the pub. They went through their pockets and discovered they had only the price of a nip each. Then they saw Erchie coming round the corner, and Erchie was well known to have fuller pockets than the two of them.

"Says I to Sandy: 'Come into the pub, quick, and gie me the price o' your nip.' He did what I tellt him and I handed it owre to the barman and ordered a dram and twa extra glasses. Then I put the three glasses along the coonter and poored the dram into the second glass and then into the third glass, and juist at that, in stepped Erchie.

"Says I: 'Hullo, Erchie, we were juist haein' a dram, and we saw ye comin', sae we ordered yin up for ye. Sandy and me's juist had oors.'

" 'Oh, thanks,' said Erchie. 'Weill, guid health, chaps,' and he dooned that dram in one gulp. And ye should hae seen Sandy's face. But Erchie ordered us up a dram each, along wi' his-sel, and we a' drank thegither and Erchie said cheerio.

"Says I to Sandy: 'Ye see, it worked!'

" 'Ay,' says Sandy: 'but, man, it was an awfu' risk!' "

Will Fyffe, who followed Neil Kenyon as a character comedian, was in fact a straight actor turned comic. He was the son of one of the last of the barnstormers, the men who took their companies round in fit-ups— penny gaffs or, as we called them in Scotland from the word "gegg" meaning a fool or an object of fun, penny geggies—or hired local halls to bring culture to the country folk. The culture might tend to consist mainly of *East Lynne* and melodrama, but occasionally they played Shakespeare, if it were only *Hamlet* and *Richard the Third* for the sake of the murders. Will Fyffe was not the comic who wanted to play Hamlet: he was the Hamlet who ended up playing the comic.

His actor training—even if it was not in any recognised Royal Academy of Dramatic Art—was evident in the technique of his Scotch comedian-ship. There is no doubt whatever that, while he could never be the singer that Lauder was, he was a better comedian, and much closer to reality in his presentation of both rural and urban Scottish types of modern times. While Lauder was happy in his role of the stage Scotchman, Fyffe got home to his audience with his commentary on the changing social scene.

That famous Secretary of State, Tom Johnston, used to tell me a story of Will Fyffe's father visiting Kirkintilloch with his company. Johnston and other local lads had discovered a way of climbing into the hall and by-passing the box-office. In the middle of a big scene, Fyffe Senior, dressed as King Claudius, stepped forward and addressed the audience with these words: "This house is full, and there is exactly nine shillings and threepence in the kitty. How the hell is it done?" It was in such a hard school that Will Fyffe learned to humour an audience.

He started to work in revue with Sybil Arundale when that form of entertainment had begun to take over from vaudeville. While he was making a living as a supporting player in this way he happened to get an idea for an act which he thought would appeal to a Scotch comedian.

He was in the Central Station in Glasgow and was engaged in conversation with a genial and demonstrative drunk who was laying off about Karl Marx and John Barleycorn with equal enthusiasm. Will asked him: "Do you belong to Glasgow?" With a broad smile, the drunk replied: "At the moment, at the moment, Glasgow belongs to me."

Will went home to his digs with the phrase echoing in his head. Like Harry Lauder, who was inspired to write *I Love a Lassie* by a chance remark from a stage-door keeper, and *Roamin' in the Gloamin'* by seeing a couple passing in the twilight on the river bank near Glasgow, Fyffe worked a phrase up to a song which has sometimes been mistakenly regarded as the Scottish National Anthem. At the same time he worked out a routine—two verses and chorus, and patter before the concluding refrain. He could not find a Scotch comedian interested enough to try it, but one night he was called on as a substitute for an act, and put it on all by himself.

About the end of the Second World War, Edwin Muir, the famous Scottish poet and translator (with his wife Willa) of *Jew Suss* and other Continental classics, asked me through to Edinburgh to give a lecture to Polish exiles on Scottish humour. I went round the music shops of Sauchiehall Street and adjacent streets gathering all the gramophone records I could lay my hands on, chiefly of Lauder, Harry Gordon and Will Fyffe. Apart from speculating how the performance would go down with the Poles, I wondered how Edwin Muir, a highbrow if ever there was one, would react to Scotch comics, who had been roundly condemned by his fellow-highbrow, Hugh MacDiarmid. (MacDiarmid despised their "chortling wut," and declared that Mae West was much more original).

Muir was not, in fact, greatly impressed by Lauder or Gordon, but he laughed until he almost cried at Will Fyffe's *I Belong to Glasgow*. "That's real," he said.

Muir had worked in Glasgow as a young man and knew the type Fyffe was representing. I think he was tickled also by the subtle satire on Marxism, for Muir had encountered a lot of muddled "proletarian" polemics in his time.

Will Fyffe's famous song and patter have formed a party piece for many an amateur comic. I have to confess that when I am stuck for something to entertain guests I fall back on this great act, which naturally I do not perform with Fyffe's skill but which still wins laughs by the sheer excellence of its script. The phrases are unforgettable—"One or two pals o' my ain," "We went in a hotel and did very well," "And that is the reason I'm fou," "There's nothing in being teetotal and saving a shilling or two," and the supreme virtue of drink in that it equips a man to speak back to his wife!

"Ay, and that's right. When a man takes a drink, he's a man. When ye're teetotal—Ach!"

No one can quite imitate the disgust with which Fyffe used that expletive "Ach!" It was the supreme expression of thirst and frustration. Only a Scot or a German can use this expletive with full effect, and no other monosyllable can say as much. We have no need of four-letter words with this three-letter one.

"When ye're teetotal," Fyffe continued, giving the temperance crusader's word a lift into a higher register, and then letting his voice fall into the depths of despondency, "ye've got a rotten feeling that everybody's your boss." This led him into a James Joycean parody of Marx's class-conscious doctrine, condemning "blooming capitalists, millionaires" in a series of spoonerisms: "I may be under the affluence of incohol but I'm not so think as you drunk I am," "Pointing the skinger of forn at the poor Glasgow working-man going home intosticated," and winding up with the challenging question: "Why! What's the poor fellow going to do? He's got to get home." The capitalists, he pointed out, went past in their cars so fast that nobody knew whether they were drunk or sober. Ah, but *he* knew, because—because—and this was the queue for the orchestra and the final chorus with which he staggered off the stage. He was a most realistic drunk. It was great acting as well as first-class music-hall.

Fyffe had so many little touches, the way he swayed, the way he took out his pipe and struggled to fill it, the way he felt in all his pockets for his matches, the way he scattered them and the way he wasted them lighting his pipe, letting them burn out in his hand while he expostulated with gestures and the "slow burn" or "double take" of his expression as he realised the match was out. He could knock his audience over with such tricks.

In other scenes he could play them up with sentiment, with a tear in his eye, and then demolish them with an anti-climax. "Ay," he would say, as a ploughman, "Tibbie's dead." When he had caught the audience's throats with the glitter of his eye and the sob in his voice, he would add: "The best whippet in Midlothian." More than any other Scotch comic he was supreme in timing.

His other warmly remembered act is his *Ninety-Four Today*. Incidentally, Fyffe's make-up in these character parts was superb, and, probably again because of his actor training, he could make a most convincing little old man. Here again were song and patter in which exaggeration served to underline reality.

This was perhaps a descendant of Pantaloon from old pantomime and, farther back, from the Commedia dell'Arte, but it was a Pantaloon with a peculiarly Scottish twist—a defiant old man from the rural background where many people really do live, and keep all their faculties, to a ripe old age.

Despite the baldness, the gaps in the teeth and the slight crack in the voice, this was a nonagenarian very sure of himself and not at all inclined to take a back seat. "I'm getting married on Thursday, though I'm ninety-four today," went the song, and at the end of the next verse:
"There'll maybe be a christening yet, before I'm ninety-five."

This could have been a rather smutty act about a dirty old man, but the Lauder, Kenyon, Fyffe brand of Scots comedians were noted for their cleanness. They won their audiences in an age that was far removed from the permissiveness of today, when even a Marie Lloyd, who was considered about the broadest, had to depend on "insinuendoes" rather than on coming right out with it. You could be funny about sex, but only in the nicest possible way. Will Fyffe's garrulous and cock-of-the-walk old man suggested virility without going into details. His boldest stroke was his tearful remembrance of his late wife—"juist a lassie when she died—seeventy—ah, but the baby lived!"

After going over his superannuated family—the one of sixty, "I saw him doon the road on his scooter. I don't think I'll ever be able to rear that lad somehow" (the one of sixty-five was "beginning to turn out a bit of a nut"), the old man took the audience into his confidence and explained the real reason why he was getting married again. He had overheard the "boys" discussing how long it would be before he kicked the bucket, and how much he was likely to leave them; and his marriage was designed to do them out of their heritage—or, as he put it, "And that's why I'm getting married again. It isn't love, ye know. Spite!"

Another of his great characterisations was the guard on the train, only slightly reminiscent of one of Dan Leno's acts, again a masterpiece of make-up, looking very dumpy and wild-whiskered in his Highland Railway uniform and fingering his whistle: "I hope it's all right. I tellt my wife to put a proper pea in it this time. Yesterday she had run oot o' peas, and she only had split peas. Silly bizzim, she pit one o' they in it, and I only got the train half-started."

He recalled the English visitor who mistook him for a porter, and shouted from the window: "Is it raining, porter?" " 'No,' says I, 'it's raining water.'

"Oh," he added, "ye've got to be fly for them. There was one the other day when the train was running along at its steady three miles an hour, and he tried to be funny. He said: 'I say, guard' "—Fyffe enjoyed imitating the English and American accents—" 'could I get out to pick a few flowers on the embankment while the train is in motion?' Oh, I was leerie for him. I said: 'If ye look oot, ye'll see there's nae flooers on this embankment.' 'Oh, that's all right,' said he, 'I've brought a packet of seeds.' "

Fyffe's song about the guard was yet another with a catchy lilt and an amusing lyric with special appeal to Scots, but perhaps also with a good deal of appeal to strangers who had experienced the humours of rail travel in the North. It had the lovely line, about his sitting at his ease in the old guard's van, "sitting in the corner on the soor-dook can." No doubt, in the South, Will Fyffe would translate that into English. "Soor-dook" is Scots for buttermilk, itself a nostalgic image.

Like Lauder, Fyffe was careful to modify his Scots tongue for London audiences. "Dear auld Glasgow toon" became "Dear old Glasgow town," "roon an' roon" became "round and round," and so on. He was out to entertain, not to give examples of dialect, but he always kept enough of the accent to identify himself and achieve the maximum of amusement.

Although his acts were so carefully prepared and presented, he was always glad of a chance for the impromptu. One night he was in a London music-hall after there had been a break-in at a Wembley international,

47

and he said to the audience: "By the way, all those hundreds of people that got into Wembley for nothing today—they weren't all Scotchmen!" Needless to say, this brought the house down.

Fyffe was in his heyday when radio was in its infancy and TV was still a long way off. His popular medium besides the stage was the gramophone, but he did have a considerable career on the talking screen, as his acting ability coupled with his flair for comedy took the fancy of producers. He was particularly good in partnership with Will Mahoney, the American acrobatic droll, and they did a funny golfing scene together.

I remember seeing Will Fyffe after he had taken part in an early British talkie which was rather a disaster—a vaudeville film made up of scenes and individual turns, including a knockabout sketch in which Anna May Wong, the Chinese actress, appeared scantily clad (for those days) and in an incongruous blonde wig. Will Fyffe told me how he sat at the back of the auditorium when the film was first put on in Leicester Square. He heard the comments of the audience, and he felt very depressed. "I sneaked oot wi' my coat collar up," he said: "I was feared I micht be recognised."

But in fact his own contribution to the picture was nothing to be ashamed of. At least, when I saw it in Edinburgh, Will's brief appearance and his topical song were to me the only part of the film worth seeing and hearing. He sang about "the price of food," meaning Scotch, and the doleful chorus was "It's twelve and a tanner a bottle." That was considered a lot to pay for a quart of whisky in the early thirties.

Arthur Askey tells a good story about Fyffe's impromptu wit. Seeing Will with his arms stretched out, wee Arthur shouted: "You never caught a fish that size." Fyffe replied: "If it was your size, I'd throw it back."

A Scotch comedian who was almost as popular as Lauder and Fyffe, as a gramophone turn, in the thirties, was Willie McCulloch of Paisley. I am glad that Kenneth McKellar has brought back the McCulloch monologues. McCulloch was a rates collector who took to the stage with his original act and toured as far south as London. His records were in great demand and became party pieces for many of us in the twenties and thirties.

I liked his old sweetie-wife character, gossiping to the customers at the same time as she condemned gossiping in others—a very real Scottish type. Some of McCulloch's jokes are unforgettable and still funny, however often one hears them. The girl who had her photo taken— "They couldna get her feet in, but it was juist as well, poor lassie—her bits were lettin' in gey bad at the time."

There was another reference to feet, the girl going to the chiropodist: "Still, it's nice to think her feet are in the hands o' a weill-kent face."

And there was the sweetie-wife's objection to the couple she heart at night courting on the landing outside her flat door: "Whis-whis-whispering to a' 'oors, that ye canna get a wink o' sleep; and the warst o' it is, they speak that low, ye canna hear a word they're saying."

On the discs, McCulloch introduced his stories in a polite Scots-English, which was itself a joy to hear, and then lapsed into broader dialect and into several changes of voice. Kenneth McKellar enjoys reproducing this voice humour of McCulloch's.

Also, more in the character comedian line than dependent on song and tartan was Jack Radcliffe, though he could sing and wear a kilt when the show called for it. If Will Fyffe was an actor using all his art to become a complete comedian, Jack Radcliffe hungered to act, and he liked nothing better than to do a realistic sketch as a drunken beach-comber. Sometimes one felt he carried his melodramatic histrionics to inordinate lengths: one felt like saying, "All right, Jack, we know you can play drunk beachcombers: you've made your point—get back to the comedy!" Which he would do eventually, when he had coaxed some-one to buy him a drink, and he held up the glass in an unsteady hand and, with a glittering eye, intoned: "Drink! You killed my father, you killed my mother. Revenge!" and drank it off. When plans were afoot to make the film *Shipbuilders*, based on George Blake's realistic novel about the Clydeside workers in the Depression, Jack Radcliffe made it known that he would dearly love to play the main character part of a riveter, but the chance did not come his way. But he did well as the minister in Geordie.

He was a grand revue artiste and put over a number of good sketches with the help of Helen Norman, a niece of the great "magical" showman, hypnotist and dealer in electrical stage effects, Dr Walford Bodie. I shall have more to say about Helen later on, as she has been one of the great female troupers of the Scottish light-entertainment scene.

5

Clowns in
the Doric

QUITE a large contingent of Scotch comedians breaks away from both
the kilted singer tradition of Harry Lauder and the character comedian
line of Neil Kenyon and Will Fyffe. These are the Scotch comics proper,
and they are almost all Glaswegians. Their humour is sheer clowning.
Indeed, some of them have modelled themselves quite consciously on th
clowns of a tradition which went back to the Middle Ages and was
active in Scotland when Sir David Lyndsay wrote his *Thrie Estaites*.
The tradition came back to Britain under the influence of the Italian
Commedia dell'Arte and it is evident in the clowns of the Elizabethan
theatre. It returned in strength early last century under the influence of
the French revival led by the Bohemian-born Jean Gaspard Deburau,
whom Jean-Louis Barrault played as a character in the Carné-Prévert
film, *Les Enfants du Paradis*. Joe Grimaldi adapted the tradition to
Cockney pantomime.

These influences are difficult to recognise in their effects on the British
stage. Both Scotland and England have a tendency to modify anything
they borrow from abroad by blending them with their own national
products. So it is with comedy. The highly artistic miming of a Deburau,
by the time it reaches Scotland, has become something quite different.

The improvisations of the Commedia dell'Arte, and its stock characters also, became likewise transmuted to something much more British—and in our case Scottish—by evolution through the Christmas pantomime. Pantaleone, the clown's butt in the Harlequinade, "the lean and slippered Pantaloon," as Shakespeare called him, became the funny old man as a favourite character of comedians.

Pedrolino or Pierrot, from being a character in mime, became any seaside entertainer in a poky hat, performing on or near a pier, or at least at the seaside, till eventually even the white slops and pom-poms were abandoned and yachting fashions or sailor suits were substituted.

The romance of Pierrot, Columbine and Harlequin was transformed into the song and dance of principal boy and principal girl in a fortuitous fairy-tale setting, but the knockabout cantrips of the Harlequinade were translated into the buffoonery of acrobatic drolls and red-nosed comedians.

In the Edwardian period the principal boy became the chief attraction of the pantomime. It was an opportunity for a pretty actress to display herself in breeches and tights at a time when women were overclad and men wanted to see more of them. Nowadays when girls in minis and tights display more even than an Edwardian principal boy, it is difficult to see what all the fuss was about; but the older generation can remember when glittering postcards of panto stars were eagerly purchased and pasted up on picture screens—the principal boys were the pin-up girls of the years up to the Great War.

War service and munition work dispelled some of the mystery that surrounded the Edwardian woman. After the war, hair and skirts got shorter, and the interest in the shapely principal boy, with her egg-timer figure and her slappable thighs, waned. The comic, rather than the glamorous actress, became the star of the pantomime. This was particularly the case in Glasgow, where the Christmas pantomimes ran late into the spring, with bus and train parties, from the surrounding countryside and farther afield, ordering their groups of seats months in advance.

Chief of the theatres in pioneering this popular appeal of the funny pantomime was the Princess's at Gorbals Cross, where George West held the fort for over twenty years as the uncrowned king of so-called "Christmas and New Year" shows, which were still blooming when the snowdrops and crocuses had bloomed and withered.

Glasgow not only developed panto in which the comic was the star but also created a public insistence that the comic should be "real Glasgow." Edinburgh might prefer well-known comedians up from London—Billy Merson, for instance—but Glasgow developed its own

51

brand of comic, and eventually Edinburgh succumbed to the same humorous appeal. Glasgow comedians became much in demand for even the high-class Edinburgh panto, their robust humour contrasting all the more comically with the refinement which the capital affects to demand in its shows.

Earlier in their careers, it was difficult to imagine either Tommy Lorne or Tom Cable as stars of the Edinburgh King's panto, but it came to pass.

These men were clowns. They were more closely related to Joe Grimaldi and the Augustes of the circus than to the Lauders or the Fyffes. They even painted themselves up like clowns. Every clown of the sawdust ring has his own characteristic make-up, in which he hopes to establish a kind of copyright. This was the case with the Glasgow comic.

Bert Denver, one of the pioneers of the brand of stage comedy based on sheer clowning, consciously modelled himself on the French mimes and painted his face like one of them. He added the Scotch effects of a Glengarry bonnet and a plaid suit and sometimes a kilt.

Ths kilt, with the Glasgow comic, tended to become clownishly short, and the tartan rather loud. With long-legged Tommy Lorne, the High-lander's proudly gartered hose became a pair of bobby socks, and when Tommy bent to putt in a golfing scene, with his back to the audience, the brevity of his kilt led his feed to turn him round. The Glasgow comic was not ashamed to convert the Highland dress into a comedy prop, or to play up to the English idea that there is something essentially funny, and perhaps even suggestive, about the kilt—an idea not entirely foreign to the urban masses of Edinburgh and Glasgow, despite the popularity of the Glasgow Highlanders and the Dandy Ninth. The Lowland Scots were laughing at Highland attire away back in the sixteenth century.

Like Bert Denver, Tommy Lorne dressed in clownish attire and painted his face white. His lankiness made him even more of a natural clown than Denver, who was a plumper type. Lorne also happened to have a funny face, with high cheek bones, hollow cheeks, and a wide mouth which needed very little exaggeration with a touch of red paint. With his pasty face, streaked eyes, and clown's wig, he accentuated the drollery with which he had been born, and which must have made him the playground butt in his days at school. I cannot rid myself of my theory that clowns are both born and made—born to excite laughter and made by the laughter they excite in their formative years. Lorne must have been a very funny overgrown schoolboy, and the "divert" of the classroom and the playground. He continued to be a perpetual "divert" on the stage.

Tommy Morgan, a boisterous Clydesider who rose from seaside entertainment to big city show business, and brought cheer to the industrial masses.

Jack Radcliffe was the Yorick who wanted to play Hamlet. Some of his characterisations teetered on the edge of melodrama, but he always finished with a laugh.

Jack Anthony ("Nae Bother at A'") started as a light comedian but adopted a clown's make-up when he turned to Scotch comedy. He was popular for his genial and kindly humour.

"Scotland's Gentleman" — Alec Finlay—is now the doyen of our Scotch comedians, singer, dancer, bagpiper, comic and sheer entertainer in the Lauder tradition.

Of course, these Glasgow comics were not proper mimes. The whole point of miming, as we have learned again from *Les Enfants du Paradis* and the visits of Marcel Marceau, was that the clown must tell his story without words. The Glasgow comic spoke, and yet his comedy remained largely visual. Tommy Lorne's speech was spasmodic, in a high, cracked, strangled voice. He spoke almost entirely in expletives and incomplete phrases. "In the name!" was one of his favourites. He could make an audience laugh by letting his feed do almost all the talking. For instance, in a scene where he was the husband not only tied to his wife's apron strings but actually wearing her apron, and washing the dishes with disastrous effect, he could achieve side-splitting effects by merely saying: "Is that what they tell ye, hen?" and turning suddenly to break a saucer on the kitchen tap.

Looking back on Lorne, one remembers not the jokes but the laughter. He was the funniest man on the stage at that time, in the years between the wars, and he held his pre-eminence until his sudden death. What he said to make us laugh is almost impossible to remember: it was rather the way he said it. He was not the maker of memorable wisecracks. One recalls him as a dame describing a charabanc ride and a hair's-breadth escape with "I thought I was gonny be hurled into maternity." But it was the strangled voice rather than the words that one carried away from the theatre. That and the bewildered wide-mouthed face. Years afterwards people thought they were paying high praise to Duncan Macrae when they said: "He's just like Tommy Lorne." Duncan, who was a trained actor, never quite appreciated that, and indeed, although there was a lot of physical resemblance, even to the wide mouth, the two were quite different. Duncan could use words: Lorne had no need of them.

I remember him in a scene outside a Monte Carlo casino. Lorne in evening dress was funny enough, but Lorne with a pistol at his head, croaking: "I'm ruined!" was somehow killingly funny. He could be quite as devastating, as a ballroom doorman, in a red uniform and polished buttons, trying to keep "fly men" from getting in for nothing, or as a tram conductor being pestered by too clever passengers.

Tommy Lorne was born in Kirkintilloch, but qualified for comedy by being brought up in the New City Road district of Glasgow, where George West was his schoolmate and playmate and his partner in go-as-you-please turns on the perilous stage of the Cowcaddens Grand Theatre, one of the roughest houses in a tough theatrical city. English comics who thought Glasgow Empire was a hard nut to crack had never been at the Grand.

55

Tommy was born Hugh Corcoran. He worked in a barber's shop. Early in the Great War of 1914-18 he managed to get on to a concert party tour with Harry McKelvie, who became the theatrical mogul of the Gorbals. Tommy went off to the war and served in India, where he entertained the troops as well as doing his khaki stint.

Harry McKelvie inherited the Princess Theatre in the Gorbals, and started Tommy there in pantomime when he was demobbed in 1918. He worked with that great old-timer, Bret Harte, an improviser with the spirit of a Commedia dell'Arte buffoon within him. Possibly Harte passed on to Tommy something of the tradition of the clowns who could walk on unrehearsed, make people laugh, and keep them in stitches.

Lorne was so Glasgow in his utterances that it was considered venturesome to put him on in Julian Wylie's production of *Goody Two Shoes* at Edinburgh King's in 1926, but Julian Wylie knew what he was doing. Lorne was funny enough visually to evoke laughter even from those who could not make out everything he said, if he was indeed saying anything.

He was such a success that he appeared in three more Julian Wylie pantos at the same theatre, and when Howard and Wyndham took control of the King's along with Glasgow Theatre Royal in 1929, they signed Lorne up for pantos in both theatres. In between, he did summer shows and tours. He even ventured into England, where it has to be admitted he was less of a success.

In 1934, he ran his own summer show at Dunoon and his own panto at Inverness, Edinburgh and Glasgow. He followed at Edinburgh with a revue, *Oh Jings!* but took ill, dying of double pneumonia, in April 1935, at the age of 45, when he had just secured a fresh two-year contract from Howard and Wyndham.

Even more sensational than Lorne's appearance in Number One dates was the choice of little Tom Cable as a King's panto star. Up till then, Cable had been part of a quite corny double act, "Cable and Carr," relying largely on the "I say, I say, I say" routine. The variant with Tom Cable was that he put his routine on as if it was a rehearsal, stopping his wife, Dot Carr, in the middle of her feeding of the cue lines, with "Wait a minute—we'll try that again!"

He would say: "Now you just stand there, and I'll come walking on again."

He would repeat his entrance, with embarrassed gestures, his hand up at his chin or his lips, as he looked apprehensively at the audience; and then swagger on with a ridiculous swing of his arms. He was petite, grotesquely pale-faced and eye-lined, and with a shock wig. He was as child-like as Harry Langdon. Yet his pantomime appearance was the talk of the town, though his triumph was rather brief. One remembers his fatuous party piece at the pantomime ball, a limerick recited as by a shy boy at the Band of Hope:

> "There was a young man of Uphall
> Who went to a fancy-dress ball:
>   He thought he would risk it
>   And go as a biscuit,
> But a dog ate him up in the hall."

He could put over such corny stuff and get away with it.

His rise was quite spectacular. He was appearing as a turn between films at La Scala in Edinburgh's Nicolson Square in 1919 for 17 a week, but was marked by the manager as "Very good;" and returned to the same "electric theatre," in 1921, for £12. Very shortly after, he was starring in a Howard and Wyndham show. He ended his days in Canada.

The childish, or child-like, line which Tom Cable cultivated was a feature of the comedy of Dave Willis. Despite his little black moustache, Willis was always the wee boy—characteristic in football jersey as a "Leith Walk Dribbler."

A good deal of Willis's capering was that of the cheeky wee boy. His chimpanzee walk, with his knees drooping, and his arms swinging so that the hands almost touched the floor, was very much what a youngster would do after a visit to the Zoo.

Years after Willis had perfected it, we saw it performed on the screen by Bob Hope and Bing Crosby, dressed up in space suits made for chimpanzees. I do not suggest that the film folk got the idea from Willis, but these internationally known entertainers were no better, and no funnier, as chimps, than Dave.

There was small-boy cheek, rather than malice, in his burlesque of Mahatma Ghandi. It was the time when the Mahatma was very much in the news, and especially in the illustrated papers, in his dhoti, leading a goat, on his spectacular visit to London. Willis managed to perform that feat of the comic impersonator, suggesting his butt while remaining very much himself, and he sang an impudent song with the lines:

> "Ye look a galoot
> In your wee dish cloot;
> Ye'd look far better
> In a plus-four suit."

In those days, "plus-fours" were still being worn by sporting types, and often by foreigners wishing to look British. Willis reckoned without the Indians in our midst, who regarded Ghandi as a sacred figure not to be joked about, and who probably resented almost as much the slighting reference to a traditional and revered style of dress. One day he was stopped outside Edinburgh's General Post Office, at the East End of Princes Street, and found himself surrounded by a group of angry Indian students. They told him to drop his impersonation of Ghandi, or he would find himself and the Theatre Royal in serious trouble. So much for what Willis regarded as one of his innocent, characteristic, *enfant terrible* pranks.

He was attacked also when he put on his caricature of Adolf Hitler. Willis, like Chaplin, saw that he was physically equipped to burlesque the German Chancellor. His Hitler act preceded *The Great Dictator*, and was screamingly funny to us at the time, when we were still at peace but when the little man in Berlin was breathing malevolently down our necks.

Dave had a good small-boy line in his patter: "I've always wanted to be a dictator: I was good at dictation at school." His song was *I'm Getting More Like Hitler Every Day*.

Well, just as there were Indian students, there were German students at our Scottish Universities, and some of them were *Hitlerjugend*, and aggressively Nazi. One of them booked a seat in a box abutting on the stage, and, when Dave came on as Hitler, this youth stood up and started a commotion in the auditorium, giving the Nazi salute, shouting: *"Heil Hitler!"* and threatening to leap on to the stage and do the comedian an injury. He was led away still shouting to the effect that Hitler would settle Dave's hash one day soon.

Just around this time, Dave was visiting the Waverley Market Carnival an Edinburgh seasonal show developed by Sir Edward Moss, of Moss' Empires, and later by Fred Lumley, a local showman and sports outfitter. Willis was introduced to one of the monkeys in the circus which was put on in the middle of the carnival, and, when the comedian grinned, the animal probably mistook the baring of teeth as a menacing expression. It flew at the comedian and bit him. Dave had to be carried off to the Royal Infirmary for an anti-tetanus injection.

When I spoke to him on that occasion, Willis said: "They tried to tell me the monkey had been frightened by one of the sea-lions. But I think it just didn't like my face. I was too like Hitler."

Dave was a Glasgow man—from the New City Road district which produced many of the typical West of Scotland comics—but he was extremely popular in Edinburgh and liked to claim a family connection with the capital, or at least with its seaside village, Portobello, of which Sir Harry Lauder was a native. He told me his mother had lived in a but-and-ben near the one in Bridge Street where Lauder was born. "I'm half Portie and half Welsh," he used to say.

His father was a Welshman, and Dave's real surname was Williams. He had the dark Celtic features and the small stature of the "Keltiberian." He was not such a neatly proportioned figure as Chaplin. He had a bigger head, and was rather gnome-like, like many another wee man on the Celtic fringe. I wrote of him in rhyme in the *Glasgow Evening News* when he appeared in panto (*Goldilocks* in Glasgow Theatre Royal) at the start of the Second World War:

> " . . . . . . germ of joy,
> The comic muse without alloy;
> His cantrips and his happy chaff
> Are only meant to make you laugh;
> His wee moustache, his glinting eye,
> His hands up-raised—'way up a 'ky—
> Have made him Dux of laughter's school,
> Although 'it makes him feel a fool.'
> As ever, Dave is up to date:
> At A.R.P. advice he's great,
> And in his battledress—Militia—
> He'd be a treat for Hore-Belisha.
> In many a fantastic scene,
> Yon flashing smile reveals its sheen;
> And, ere the end, the wise and grave
> Are rendered just as daft as Dave."

The Militia had been formed to facilitate the intake of young fellows into the Forces, and as usual Dave made an amusing skit out of it. There are two of his catch phrases in that old rhyme of mine. It was his infant son Denny (now a widely known comedian) who used to say: "Daddy's in an aeroplane, 'way, 'way up a 'ky," Dave having been in the Royal Flying Corps in the Great War; and it was a phrase the wee comic used repeatedly, with appropriate gestures and baby voice and expression—again an example of his childlikeness.

Also, when his capers led him into an embarrassing situation and the audience were enjoying it, he would say bashfully: "It makes you feel such a fool." Denny Willis is unlike his father in many respects. He is taller for one thing, he is blond, and he wears pince-nez and no moustache in his favourite clown character. But he resembles his father in his good comedy timing, his tumbling, and his apologetic manner—"So sorry"— as he wrecks the routine of the male-voice choir.

Dave Willis grew up as a comic in the period when the screen was becoming a growing challenge to the living theatre, and when show promoters were balancing the prospects of cinema and the stage. There was a spell when films were a novelty introduced into vaudeville programmes, before it was fully realised that the flickering image was the cuckoo in the next. Moss' Empires and other variety houses featured the American Bioscope, usually newsreels, from about the beginning of the century.

By 1908, the cinemas which had proliferated were becoming extremely popular, but variety acts were able to survive as turns between films. Dave Willis appeared on the stage in more than one "electric theatre" of the early movie era. Pringle's Picture Palace was one of them. It had its grand opening in Edinburgh's Elm Row (part of Leith Walk) on November 16, 1908, presented by Ralph Pringle's "North American Animated Picture Company and high-toned varieties" (gallery 2d, circle 3d, pit 4d, stalls 6d). The theatre is now Scottish Television's colour studios.

Even in those days the movies were striving to break out of their silence. Picturehouses in 1910 were featuring song recitals on the animatophone. Harry Lauder was miming on the screen to the accompaniment of his songs on the gramophone. Edison's Kinetophone was giving us early "talkies" in 1914. Some cinemas featured elocutionists talking alongside melodrama on the screen. I can still hear the villain's blood-curdling laugh.

But the cinema development which had the biggest impact in the days leading up to the Great War was the comedy element represented by Keystone, and John Bunny and Flora Finch (a fat man and skinny woman act very much akin to what was seen on the variety stage) in Vitagraph. Keystone specialised in burlesque of melodrama, even of the melodrama which had spilled over on to the screen in series like *The Exploits of Elaine*. There was a close affinity between Keystone and the British music-hall drollery associated with the name of Fred Karno, a feature so popular in 1914 that our men marched to war singing:

> "We are Fred Karno's Army—
> What bloody use are we?"

60

to a familiar hymn tune. It was natural that Mack Sennet and Hal Roach should seek the transfer of some of Fred Karno's talented artistes, such as Charles Chaplin, Stan Laurel and Billy Ritchie.

Chaplin was often in Scotland as a variety act, early on as probably the best of J. W. Jackson's Eight Lancashire Lads and *Casey Court*, and later as one of Fred Karno's leading comics. In 1909 Chaplin was in Scotland, in Moss' Empires, in a Fred Karno sketch called *The Football Match*. The star was Harry Weldon as "Stiffy the Goalkeeper," and Chaplin was the chief supporting comic after Will Poluski, Junior. But it was after Karno had taken *Mumming Birds* to New York, and Mack Sennet had lured away his best mime apart from Fred Kitchen (who was getting too old to start a film career), that we really began to notice Chaplin.

Until we saw the little bowler-hatted character in *Mabel's Dilemma* (a Mabel Normand picture), our favourite cinema comedian was Fatty Arbuckle. The Chaplin craze started in 1914, and roared through 1915. Cut-outs of Chaplin with his cane and fag-end were standing at cinema doors. Mamie Souter, on our Scottish music-halls, started to sing *The Moon Shines Bright on Charlie Chaplin*, and everybody was putting on a bowler hat, taking up a swagger cane, and imitating Chaplin. Jack Edge was doing it in a touring revue, *Search Me*, which came to Scotland in August 1915. The best "Chaplin" I saw was Stanley Lupino, in *This Is The Life*, two months later, but then all the Lupinos were superb at acrobatic drollery and burlesque.

In another revue, *Watch Your Step*, that autumn of 1915, there was a feature called *Chaplin Feet*, with a tap dance in the splay-footed style under a flickering light. There were shows with Chaplin double acts, and some where the entire female chorus danced in Chaplin costume. And cinemas were offering prizes for the best impersonations of the bowler-hatted tramp. One of the prize-winners was a young Serviceman called Dave Willis.

I am sure Willis learned a lot from studying Chaplin, though he added to the traditional miming and visual comedy the Scotch touches—the broad tongue and the playground phrases and "stotting-rhyme" songs. Indidentally he played Pringle's as a struggling artist, and years later, in 1961, he was back at the same theatre (by now the Edinburgh Gateway) in legitimate drama, *The Comic*, by Maurice Fleming. That was after Dave had retired and made several spasmodic comebacks. He had £100,000 when he gave up the stage in 1952 and invested his savings in hotel-keeping (rather a mantrap for comedians). In 1954 he was broke, and, as a man of 60, played Dame for the first time in panto, in Aberdeen. It was a sad business for him to have to shave off the moustache which had been a part of his stage persona during his highly paid career.

He really got going in the twenties and thirties, although as late as 1924 he was playing second comic in *Robinson Crusoe* to Mark Denison: he was "Boosey the Mate" to Denison as "Will Atkins" in a pantomime written by George West, a Glasgow show which toured the other towns.

It was the *Half Past Eight* and *Five Past Eight* summer shows started by Howard and Wyndham early in the thirties in Glasgow and Edinburgh which, with revue and pantomime, built Willis up into a great star. His fame lasted through the war years and into the fifties, when cardiac trouble cut his career short: you can't tumble and caper with a bad heart. He had small pierrot shows and other engagements from time to time, and in variety revivals he put on his favourite act, the skit on the A.R.P., *In My Wee Gas Mask*: "Ye canna get in my shelter for it's far too wee . . . The finest looking warden in the A.R.P."

Another of our comics who went in for a clown type of make-up and dress (after a career as a light comedian) was Jack Anthony, who painted on large black eyebrows contrasting oddly with his blond hair. He lined his eyes, the lobes of his nose, his lips, and his chin, and wore funny wee hats and woolly coats. His playing was a romp. At times, however, he would do a Kenyon-like character act, such as the postie scene which gave him his famous catchline. He was being told how to get to a place and the directions were as involved as the way was steep. "But you'll manage all right," he was assured, to which he replied, spontaneously the first time: "Aw, nae bother at aw" in a typically Glasgow lilt which surprised him by the gust of laughter it evoked from a sympathetic audience. Like Dave Willis with his "Way up a 'ky," Anthony decided to use the line regularly. Incidentally, even the classical clown Deburau did a series of character acts, as did Dan Leno.

Like other Scotch comedians, Anthony discovered he had a public on the other side of the Atlantic and wherever there were Scots in exile. I met him in December 1954 shortly after he returned from America, where he had done a coast-to-coast tour extending to eleven weeks and including cities in both the United States and Canada. He told me: "I heard more Scots spoken over there than here. People who speak high pan when they leave Scotland start speaking Scots in the States. They take a homesick interest in the old Scots words and expressions. I was continually being asked to repeat some of my phrases for the benefit of somebody who had been away from Scotland for a long time"

He was on his way to star along with Dave Willis in the pantomime at His Majesty's, Aberdeen, in which Willis made his comeback. Jack said, "I'll enjoy working with Dave: he's a great trouper." Anthony was already running his hotel at Dunbar: he was more successful in this than poor Willis.

One thing I used to find with the old comics was the high regard they had for one another, and their cameraderie when they met or worked together. Willis and Anthony had both worked in Popplewell's Gaiety Whirls at Ayr, an enterprise which contributed greatly to the fostering of cheerful Scotch entertainment, though the Popplewells were originally from Yorkshire. These Gaiety Whirls will crop up several times in the history of our comics.

6

The Laird
of Inversnecky

MUSIC HALLS grew up in Aberdeen and Dundee as well as in Glasgow and Edinburgh and both the North-East and the Angus countryside were to contribute to the comic scene. Will Fyffe was a Dundonian, and there were several well-known comedians from Aberdeen, a city famous for its Joke Factory and for telling stories against itself.

There has been a tradition of fun in that sparkling granite city by the North Sea since the Abbot of Bon Accord ruled over its topsy-turvy festivities in the Middle Ages. It had its Alhambra Music Hall going strong at the end of last century, with Harry Clifton and May Edwards in full song, Clifton contributing "You never miss the water till the well gangs dry" as well as running the show. There was also Her Majesty's, which later became the Tivoli Music Hall (1906) and the Livermores' Jollity Vaudeville Theatre (1892-96). There was the Palace Theatre, Bridge Street. W. J. Ashcroft followed Clifton at the Alhambra. But there were also beach shows, such as Dave Thomson's Beach Pavilion, for Aberdeen is a popular seaside resort as well as a busy fishing and commercial city. Harry Gordon played at the Beach Pavilion for 26 years and from 1924 until 1940 he ran the place.

Pierrots in the North-East (I remember them at Stonehaven as well as Aberdeen) often drew their talent from south of the Border, but their mainstay was local humour. The North-East speaks a different Doric from that of Glasgow, sharper and less drawled, and the ear has to be tuned into it, even if one is Scottish. For the sake of the summer visitors the Aberdonian comics learned to modify their accents, but, like the Glaswegians, they never could resist, now and again, a characteristically local joke, often based on the dialect.

For instance, I heard a Stonehaven pierrot playing a small boy who refused to put on his school cap when told. When asked why, he replied: "It's fou o' golachs."

I am sure the English visitors laughed just at the funny sound of the words. They could hardly be expected to know that it meant the cap was full of earwigs. And many Scots would not understand it either, because the earwig is one creature which seems to change its name every five miles or so.

The greatest comedian to emerge from Aberdeen was Harry Gordon, who had a meteoric career in London (or rather the short career of a misfired rocket), but settled down much more successfully in the South of Scotland, where he could retain enough of his Aberdeen accent for identification while being able to make himself understood. He was another little man, witty in the hard and glittering granite-city manner, as well as capable of wholehearted clowning. He was so much more verbal than Tommy Lorne, George West, and Dave Willis, that he made an ideal gramophone and radio performer. The BBC liked him because he was a perfect reader, usually of his own scripts. Many comedians who go over easily with memorised scripts laced with ad libs are awkward readers, and in broadcasting until recently the script, as officially passed, was almost sacrosanct.

Gordon's songs always fitted his personality neatly. "I'm the man that maks the smoke come oot the lum," he sang as a railway fireman (like Lauder, Kenyon, Will Fyffe, and others he varied his act with character sketches from the Scottish towns and countryside). His chief of the fire brigade had some marvellous racy Aberdeen patter. "The fire's gaun oot, is't? Could ye nae keep it gaun till we get there . . . Are ye sure it's a fire? Maybe it's the man next door lichtin' his pipe: that Cooncil hooses has awfu' thin wa's . . . Na, we've owre monie fires to gang til the noo: ye'll need to send a postcaird and we'll send ye a form to fill in for an appointment."

He had great comedy timing. I recall his standing up to address a luncheon in Glasgow at which most of the guests were women. He said: "Ye'll need to excuse my wife nae being here. She had an accident: she was having her face liftit, and the crane broke."

He often played Dame in pantomime, and his dresses were magnificent, but he was just as funny in male parts. He was Buttons in a *Cinderella* panto I saw at Glasgow Alhambra early in the war, and a rhyme I wrote at the time sums up my reactions to his scintillating wit and kindly humour:

"Twinkle, twinkle, little star:
What a perfect scream you are!
Though your buttons shine so bright,
Brighter still your wit at night.
Many years now—man and boy—
You have worked to give us joy;
Also as a Dame sedate,
We have seen you scintillate.
Now you're Buttons, pert and cheery—
How could Glasgow e'er grow dreary?"

There was no question about his brilliance in this show of Tom Arnold's: he was extremely funny as conductor of a "Symphony Orchestra" (of course, the gag has been worked from time immemorial, but some do it better than others). He worked splendidly in contrasted tininess with Big Bertha Belmore, and he sang "Run, Rabbit, Run" with Muriel Barron, throwing in impersonations of Lionel Barrymore and the Western Brothers, as well as an operatic aria. He was terrific as an evacuee out to disrupt the peace of the "Big Hoose" that had taken him in. And he and Jack Holden had a great piece of front-cloth crosstalk in the old panto tradition.

He was still brilliant in the 1950s, standing up to younger comics in the Howard and Wyndham summer shows. Like Dave Willis, he had a long run in these seasonal entertainments, and was never stale.

He wrote a lot of his own songs, patter and sketches. With Tommie Connor, he wrote one song (not a comedy number), which is still sung and often requested—*Down in the Glen*—

"The sheep are in the fold
And there's peace worth more than gold
For a shepherd in that heaven
Down in the glen."

Like other comics, he knew the value of a little sentiment alternating with his jokes.

He was also an appreciative—and generously paying—user of scripts by others, if they were clever enough for the high standard Harry set himself.

One of his performances which made me laugh a lot was as a farm hand discussing the farmer and his wife. This is the theme of many a bothy ballad from the North-East—the class feeling on the farm—but Harry gave it his own individual twist. The farmer had married a former mannequin—or, as Gordon pronounced it, "mannie-quyne" (*quyne* being the common Aberdeen word for a girl). "Ye should see her feeding the hens!" and here Gordon mimed this operation, using all the simpering gestures, the walk, the twists and turns, of a model at a dress show, while obviously scattering grain to the chickens. So that despite his excellence in verbal wit, he could vary it with good visual comedy.

Gordon had great appeal to the city masses and also to the country folk, who rolled up by the bus-load to see his shows. Glasgow and Edinburgh could keep him going most of the year, with panto and summer show and he could make about £300 a week from the big dates in the 1950s, thirty years after he had first captured the South of Scotland audiences. In the autumn he would go on concert tours in Canada, Africa and the United States. This was almost a rest after a summer show in which he had to keep learning new material for complete change of programme every week or fortnight. The remarkable thing about Gordon and other leading Scotch comedians in the fifties was the way their shows held out against TV. But they could shine on TV themselves, though there, more than in the live theatre, they had a job to squeeze in among the London talent.

Except for Canada and the States, Australia and New Zealand—and South Africa, with its lack of TV—Scotch comedians became even less for export. But the best of them could make a good living on their own side of the Border and did not need the London Palladium, though making Scottish audiences laugh is a hard way of making a living. A favourite joke of the comics is "Still, it's better than working!" But they do have to earn their corn.

Charlie Kemble, the wholehearted star of the Fyfe and Fyfe entertainers at Dunoon for many hilarious years, also came from Aberdeen, but had most of his upbringing in Glasgow, where it seems most of ou comedians have to come from. He was a great trouper and trainer of troupers, and his own song, the impromptu verses about people in the audience with the refrain "Fol-ol-a-diddle-ol," which gave him a moment to think, was a real show-stopper. His rhymes were sometimes cruder than McGonagall's, but he always managed the rhythm. G. S. Melvin, who rivalled Harry Gordon in well-dressed Dame parts, was another from the East coast, a Dundonian who found his niche in London and who used to tour Scotland almost as an English comedian.

Like Charlie Kemble, Harry Gordon influenced a lot of other comics. He worked well with Jack Anthony, Alec Finlay and Jack Radcliffe, as well as with Jack Holden and Clem Ashby. And English artists remember him from his Beach Pavilion days, when he not only welcomed them as performers but saw to it that they enjoyed their stay in Aberdeen. The Laird of Inversnecky—he invented a whole series of Inversnecky characters—was one of the nicest of comics to all who met him. He was much mourned when he died in 1959.

7

Scotland's Gentleman

ONE of the modern performers who has kept up the Lauder tradition of the kilt and the repertoire of comic and sentimental song, but in a manner unique, is wee Alec Finlay, who has been prominent on Grampian Television with his show, *The Royal Clansmen*.

As a boy Alec used to imitate Lauder at concerts. He had in fact never seen Lauder, only heard him on his grandfather's Edison-Bell phonograph, but he had an idea, from hearing his elders speak, of what Lauder looked like and how he used the stage. Wee Alec donned the kilt and got hold of a funny walking stick, and he walked up and down and sang the Lauder songs, jiggled his legs at the corners of his parade and made gestures with his hands. The laughter of the grown-ups encouraged him. He was the star of Govanhill Band of Hope and the women's guilds.

He knew from then on that he was a natural entertainer, but he understood that an industrial job was necessary to make a living, so on he went into engineering like so many other young Clydesiders. As the prospects in the twenties were not too bright for engineers, however, he soon turned back to his favourite occupation, learning the business from

Charlie Kemble in the seaside shows and plunging, with his partner, Ronnie Boyd, into the music-hall and cinema variety circuits. There was still room for turns between the silent movies, especially in the Scottish cities. But the talkies finished that and also gave the music-hall a shake. Alec had by this time teamed up, matrimonially and professionally, with the Glasgow dancer, Rita Andree. Theirs was a sophisticated double act, well-dressed, in which Alec wore white tie and tails but changed into the kilt for the really Scottish numbers. Their act took the fancy of that stern critic, Sir Oswald Stoll.

On one date they discovered that Alec's evening dress trousers were missing. At Rita's suggestion, he put on his kilt with his white tie, tails and silk hat. This was when they had established themselves in the English circuits, and it gave Alec an idea when he saw the audience reaction. Later he billed himself as "Scotland's Gentleman." He toured with Ben Lyon and Bebe Daniels, and later ran pantos in Dundee and toured all over.

Alec is a master of stagecraft, and he has always been aware that a comedian must keep on the search for new material and new gimmicks. To his talent for putting over comic songs, patter, and the occasional sentimental Scots ballad, he added the accomplishment of playing the bagpipes. He even danced the Highland Fling, accompanying himself on the pipes—quite an achievement, though, as Alec said, "It was copyright by me and to me, simply because I was the only man daft enough to try it."

Recently, when the Greys' record, *Amazing Grace*, was all the rage, was all the rage, Alec scored a hit on Grampian TV playing *Abide With Me* on the pipes. This is typical of his adaptability, the reason why he won a TV award as the leading showbiz team with his Grampian series, *Alec Finlay and the Royal Clansmen*.

After 1940 Alec worked mostly in Scotland on variety tours and in pantomime. He took vaudeville to the North with great success in the years before TV invaded that area and he toured as well in T. M. Watson's *Bachelors Are Bold*, technically a "straight" play but one full of the comedy situations which one so thoroughly trained and experienced in pierrots, variety, and panto knew well how to put across.

Now he has adapted himself to the small screen, which in the 1950s threatened the living theatre in which he had grown up, and he has been able to prove that the spirit of the variety road show, in which the comedian is the leader of the revels, can be revived on TV, and that, in one way or another, what used to be called "music-hall" is determined to come back.

70

Stanley Baxter began in comedy roles in the legitimate theatre but was a natural for panto and revue. He likes to step out of the Scotch conventions and is noted for the versatility of his characters and impersonations.

Two typical appearances in the popular BBC television Stanley Baxter Show. Above, as Harry Lauder and below, Shirley Temple.

(Photographs, BBC Scotland.)

Lex McLean ("Sexy Lexy" instrumentalist, stand-up comic character comedian and performer of situation music-hall sketches, has done most to keep the spirit of old-time variety going in Scotland.
Walter Carr (left) partners him in a BBC television programme.

Commercial television in its earliest phase in Scotland turned Larry Marshall from a straight actor to a comic compere and Scotch comedian with a special flair for audience participation.

He is a thorough variety artist, bringing out all the appeal of which vaudeville was capable, with music, song comic and serious, the situation sketch, cross-talk, dancing, frolics in general and, of course, spectacle, on a scale suited to TV. In this *mélange*, Alec is in his element, singing, playing, and dancing himself, switching from a funny ditty to *The Crookit Bawbee* and occasionally putting on, reminiscent of those first juvenile attempts of his to entertain at the concert, *The Lauder Story*, in which, with more knowledge now of how the Portobello man really appeared on the stage, he gives Sir Harry's biography in song and dance.

8

Actors into Comics

I HAVE already stated that Will Fyffe had actor training, as a strolling player, before he became a revue feed and then drifted into Scotch character comedy. But the transition from the legitimate to the variety theatre has been a phenomenon more of the period following the Second World War.

Despite the closing down of theatres with the impact of TV, despite the switch of many an old variety house or cinema to bingo, both summer shows and pantomime persisted in the Scottish cities and there was a demand for new comedians. Several of them came over from straight acting, or at least from comedy acting in straight plays.

The most notable was Duncan Macrae. But Duncan, though he had played serious parts, had a predisposition to comedy. He was physically suited to clowning, with his long angular figure, high cheek bones, and twinkling eyes, his wide mouth and jutting chin.

When he played the Stuart king in Robert MacLellan's *Jamie the Saxt* in Glasgow Citizens' in 1947, the word went round: "This is Tommy

Lorne born again." Duncan, who probably had not seen much of Tommy Lorne, did not take this as a high compliment, but Lorne was a music-hall artist whom the highbrows had discovered and taken to themselves, and when they compared the two their praise of Macrae was sincere.

In fact, Macrae could mime as effectively as Lorne, but he also was able to deliver a straight script, while Lorne had the natural comedian's talent for getting laughs without any real wit in the script but would not have been at ease in a play or a character part.

Macrae was born in Glasgow in the autumn of 1905, of Sutherland crofting stock, and had a good education at Allan Glen's School and Glasgow University. He taught before studying for the stage. He performed in various Glasgow companies, semi-amateur and professional, before appearing in London at Sadler's Wells in 1945, as Donald Macalpin in *The Forrigan Reel*, by James Bridie, a playwright he greatly admired and whose plays he worked hard to keep alive. His favourite role, he used to say, was that of a "dignified fool." He created the immensely comic part of Flatterie in *The Thrie Estaites* at Edinburgh Festival in 1948 and returned to the role in 1959, at the same time appearing in late-night revue, using the part of "Jamie the Saxt" as a variety turn.

When Robert Kemp, inspired by Jouvet's performance of *L'Ecole des Femmes*, turned the Molière play into Scots for Edinburgh Gateway, Duncan Macrae played the part of Mr Oliphant. Although *Let Wives Tak Tent* had its eye on the Jouvet presentation, the character of Mr Oliphant was no slavish copy of the French actor's interpretation, but became a real Scotch comedy role, and demonstrated Macrae's great range of mime, and skill with dialogue.

Dr Tom Honeyman and others devised a pantomime for Glasgow Citizens entitled *The Tintock Cup* and based on a Lanarkshire legend and rhyme. Macrae was the natural choice for Dame and showed his aptitude for wholehearted clowning. But he was more enthusiastic for the propagation of Scottish drama, especially James Bridie's. As Harry MacGog in Bridie's *Gog and Magog*, a part based loosely on the humourless would-be poet and barnstormer, "Sir" William McGonagall, Macrae made a great hit on the Festival Fringe in 1954, in a theatre associated with some of the most robust Scotch comedians—the Edinburgh Palladium.

He alternated with Stanley Baxter in a series of Henry Sherek productions in the Lyceum in 1956, as Michael Scott in Alexander Reid's *The Warld's Wonder* (also broadcast and fortunately preserved on tape and revived recently with Macrae in the role). He was Judas in *A Man*

Named Judas; Agnes McLuckie, a comic Dame part, in Donald Mackenzie's *Rabbie Burns Slept Here*. Even as Judas Iscariot, his was a clown's role, touching on the narrow boundary between comedy and tragedy.

His excellence as a Dame brought him into the Glasgow Alhambra pantomimes in between his own enterprises, touring Scottish plays, for which he formed a partnership, called Scottishows, with the playwright, T. M. Watson.

At Edinburgh Festival time, he was as often on the Fringe as in the mainstream, and he enjoyed making sardonic comments on the official offerings. He could probably have been a great satiric actor and comedian. He was always extremely outspoken.

He appeared in several British films—*Whisky Galore* (*Tight Little Island* was its American title), *The Kidnappers, Tunes of Glory, Our Man in Havana, Casino Royale,* and *You Are Only Young Once* (from a Bridie play). He appeared at the Manhattan Centre, New York, with a concert party in 1959 and made later tours abroad. He was the comic janitor in a musical, *Skerryvore,* in 1961, at Edinburgh Empire, one of the last shows there before the theatre went over to bingo.

Macrae was as much a visual as a voice comedian, and the little that there is of him on tape does not do justice to his memory. He was not a singer but could always oblige with a folk number called *The Wee Cock Sparrow*. The original version, which I heard before Macrae made it famous again, was sung in student revues by an Edinburgh lawyer called Hugh Frater, and it went:

> A wee cock sparra sat upon a tree (*thrice*)
> And he whistled as blithe as blithe could be.
>
> By came a boy wi' his bow and arra (*thrice*)
> Says he, "I will shoot yon wee cock sparrow."
>
> The wee cock sparra said "That will never do" (*thrice*)
> And he flappit his wings and away he flew.
>
> The boy wi' the arra let fly at the sparra (*thrice*)
> And he hit a man that was hurlin' a barra.
>
> The man wi' the barra cam owre wi' the arra (*thrice*)
> Says he, "Did ye take me for a cock sparra?"
>
> The boy said, "Sir, ye'll need to excuse me (*thrice*)
> For indeed your coat tails and your neb did confuse me."

The man hit the boy on the side of the head (*thrice*)
And the boy raised a roar fit to wauken the dead.

And a' this time the wee cock sparra (*thrice*)
Was whistlin' a tune on the shank o' the barra.

Hughie Frater told me he picked the song up from an old man somewhere about Stirling. Duncan Macrae sang it "very Glasgow," and his version had significant differences from Frater's. Macrae's wee cock sparra in the first verse was "chirpin' awa as blithe as could be." The boy came by with "a bow'n an arra: Says he, 'I'll get ye, ye wee cock sparra'." But his best lines were:

The man hit the boy though he wisnae his farra
And the boy stood and glowered: he was hurt to the marra.

"Though he wisnae his farra" was real Glescaranto, a language which has been the stock in trade of all the Glasgow comics. There is a tendency in that city and in other Lanarkshire towns, such as "Murrawell" and "Ruglen," to avoid the *th* in certain words, sometimes even including the definite article which may be pronounced *ra* instead of *the*. But the avoidance is particularly common with words ending in *ther*—so *mother*, *father*, *brother*, and *other* become *murra*, *farra*, *brurra*, and *urra*. So *he wisnae his farra* means *he wasn't his father*, and one can understand the boy's indignation at this breach of the Glasgow social code.

Another of Duncan's simple folk songs on tape is his *Three Craws*.

More than Duncan Macrae, Stanley Baxter has exploited the peculiarities of Glescaranto, or as he calls it, *Parliamo Glasgow*. It is quite true that some native Glasgow speakers, especially by running the words closely together, can make it sound like a foreign language. In addition to the dialect, pronunciation peculiarities, there is the intrusion of rhyming slang, which is just as popular among the Glaswegians as among the Cockneys. In Glasgow, rhyming slang used to be known as *Macfarlane Lang* after a biscuit manufacturing firm. By slicing off the rhyming word, the usual practice with rhyming slang, it becomes simply *The Macfarlane* (or, as they pronounce it in Glasgow, *Macfaurlin*). Probably the commonest rhyming slang word used in Glasgow is *china* (*china plate* rhyming with *mate*) for a friend or companion. It was a favourite word of a Queen's panto comedian, Sam Murray, who greeted his audience with "How ya, chinas?"

Stanley Baxter made most amusing use of Glasgow's speech peculiarities in a TV series in which he played the part of a professor of linguistics explaining in elaborate English what the various phrases meant. There have been similar gags about other peculiar forms of English, *Strine* (Australian), *Noozild* (New Zealand), and *Scouse* (Liverpool), for instance. I can recall it as a joke in *Judge*, New York, about 1928, where they had illustrated lessons in wholly invented Brooklynese. No gag is entirely new, but Baxter, in Ezra Pound's phrase, made it new with his *Parliamo Glasgow* and it brought him well-deserved popularity.

Baxter's career ran alongside Duncan Macrae's as a straight actor, but he became even more involved in the comedy stage. Now 46, he is celebrated more as a comedian than as a "legitimate" player. He started in Forces radio shows in Malaya, but was keen on drama. He joined Glasgow Citizens as assistant stage manager in search of training and experience, played alongside Duncan Macrae, then the leading Citizens actor, and succeeded him in comedy parts.

His professional appearance was in the 1948 production of *The Thrie Estaites* at Edinburgh. He played a relatively small role—Correction's Varlet. In *The Tintock Cup*, which turned Macrae into a panto Dame, Stanley Baxter played a broker's man. That was in 1949.

A long contract in radio revue followd. In 1952 he had a contract with Howard and Wyndham to become the star comic of *Half Past Eight* and pantomime. His radio series with Jimmy Logan was followed by a show of his own. He was still playing comedy roles in straight drama, alternating with Macrae in that Henry Sherek series: he made a great hit as Elwood Dowd in *Harvey*, a part played by Joe E. Brown and other accomplished comics.

London saw him first at the Saville in 1959 as Sydney Green in *The Amorous Prawn*, and he played the city later in revue, *On the Brighter Side*, and toured Australia in *Chase Me, Comrade*. His films have included *V.I.P.*, *The Fast Lady*, *Crooks Anon*, and he has been even more successful on TV. Baxter is extremely versatile, a great mime and a first-class mimic. One of the cleverest things I saw him do was all three leading parts in a burlesque of *Dr Finlay's Casebook*.

Not so obvious a recruit from straight acting is Andy Stewart. He appeared in *Gog and Magog* with Duncan Macrae, and came on later at the same theatre, Edinburgh Palladium, in late-night revue (on the Festival Fringe). He sang *Ye Canna Shove Yer Granny Off a Bus* as various popular artists might render it. His impersonations included Billy Daniels and Louis Armstrong. He also told a series of funny stories.

Since then Andy has gone places, and vies with Alec Finlay as the leading exponent of the Lauder tradition, mingling song with humour and leading his own show, with dancers, musicians, and other entertainers. He married an Edinburgh Gateway actress, Sheila Prentice, whose sister was married to the dancer, Dixie Ingram. Dixie has been a great help on the spectacular side of the Andy Stewart shows. Latterly Andy has had the backing of the Bruce McClure Dancers. His own songs—especially *A Scottish Soldier*—have caught the public taste, and he has a good repertoire of traditional songs, such as *The Road and the Miles to Dundee*.

He has done some good Scotch character comedy as a Highland policeman and an Angus farm boy. As a Dundonian, like Will Fyffe, he knows the Angus countryside well. Recently he has kept up a pleasing standard in *Scotch Corner* on TV, and has been commended by viewers for the care he takes with his shows and his creditable "spruce, well-groomed appearance" in Highland dress.

It has been said of Andy Stewart by a theatre critic who must also have been a cynic: "He can't act, he can't dance: all he can do is fill theatres." The last bit of this, at least, was true of Andy as long as there were still theatres to be filled.

The hunger of panto and the summer show for new comics was responsible also for the career of Rikki Fulton, who played Edinburgh Gateway and other drama centres on his way to the revue stage. Now Fulton is back in drama, though again in a comedy part, in Duncan Macrae's old role in *The Thrie Estaites* (Edinburgh Festival 1973). He tried many openings into the entertainment industry—radio revue, radio compere, with Joe Loss's and other bands (*Show Band Show*). In Edinburgh Gateway he played a comic plumber in my *Festival City* (Fringe, 1952), and took part in a Christmas revue which led Hamish Turner to engage him for a late-night Fringe show at the Palladium. It was from this that Fulton stepped into Howard and Wyndham panto and summer show.

He was successful both as a Dame and in his team work with Jack Milroy (*Francie and Josie*). Rikki had played a Teddy Boy part in the Palladium revue with his own parody of *The Teddy Bears' Picnic* (*The Teddy Boys' Picnic*). Teddy Boys were still topical when Fulton and Milroy personified them in the *Francie and Josie* sketches and, despite the disappearance of the type, they continued to be popular in these roles with Scottish city audiences. Stan Marr's scripts were a great impetus with their comedy situations. Rikki Fulton also writes scripts.

Like many comics, he can be a rather serious character off-stage. I found him once in his dressing room at Edinburgh King's, on a couch, with his feet up high and his head lolling near the floor. I asked him if he was practising yoga. "No," he said, without the flicker of a smile, "I'm letting the blood run back into my brains."

He studies his revue comedy as seriously as any straight part he may be asked to play. Comedy, someone said, is a serious business. Rikki has the gift of comedy timing, something no comedian can really live without. No matter who writes a script, whether it is the comedian himself or someone else, only the comic can tailor it to his own personality and only the comic can make it work.

Even more of a straight actor turned comic is Walter Carr, Lex McLean's foil in the TV series. Carr is a talented player in legitimate drama, especially in naturalistic Glasgow plays. It is perhaps not such a great transition from that to the Lex McLean type of comedy, which is closely related to the human condition in the working-class areas of our cities.

Russell Hunter and Bill Simpson in the past year have been prominent in comic parts. They were the Uglies in *Cinderella* in high-class Edinburgh panto. Hunter in particular shows a great comedy talent, and has as much of a future in revue and panto as in straight drama. He seems to enjoy his opportunities in both types of entertainment.

Clem Ashby was in Perth Repertory when he succeeded Jack Holden as supporting comedian to Harry Gordon.

9

Musical Clowns

IN the careers of most comedians, music has played a significant part. The comic song in particular has been prominent in the stock-in-trade of most of them, though a Tommy Lorne, a George West, or a Duncan Macrae could dispense with it entirely. The complete comedian ought to be a minstrel as well as a jester. He should be able to dance as well, and some comics are a complete variety programme in themselves. But a few have been successful without much musical or vocal talent.

Recently I heard Arthur Askey say on radio that Lauder was less of a comedian than a concert singer while Will Fyffe was a great character comedian, and this more or less confirms my own estimate of these two contrasted Scottish entertainers. Lauder, Gordon, Finlay, and Andy Stewart have all been good comic singers and the comic song was important in music hall.

Some of our comedians have actually begun as musicians, and retained music prominently in their act. Jimmy Logan began as a pianist and so did Lex McLean.

Two Scots who have achieved some success on the comic stage are almost in the tradition of the musical clown—George Chisholm and Billy Crockett.

Variety in the good old days had quite a number of these musical acts—Grock, the Swiss clown, was perhaps the daddy of them all, but their range of zaniness was quite spectacular. There was a crazy orchestra known as the Ten Looneys. There was Vasco the Mad Musician. There was Herschel Henlere, with his exaggerated foreign accent and his references to "jizz." Chirgwin, the White-Eyed Kaffir, was a great variety act in my boyhood, with his violin, his sentimental songs—*My Fiddle is My Sweetheart* and *I Am But a Poor Blind Boy*—and that odd one-string fiddle with a thing like a bladder of lard in the middle on which he beat as on a drum. Later we have had Jimmy James and Ted Ray—and, of course, Jack Benny in the States—using the fiddle as a prop in a stand-up comic act.

George Chisholm is well known on television with his nimble trombone and his clever miming. He can be funny without uttering a sound except on his trombone, but when he does talk or sing he is a natural-born Glasgow comic, and there is a great strain of the humour of the Glasgow streets also in his miming and facial contortions. Like some other comedians, he found his metier in Forces entertainment. He was a member of the Squadronaires in the Royal Air Force, and developed his comedy there. Now he fits into all sorts of shows from the Black and White Minstrels to pantomime. The rhythmic element in his performance often heightens the comedy effect. He would have been highly acceptable to the old-time music-hall audiences.

Billy Crockett, a clever clarinetist and all-round musician, has developed the kilted comedy line and also spearheaded shows with the emphasis on both humour and music. With his individual act he has had successful tours abroad, and in the winter of 1972-73 his was one of the specialty performances in the ice pantomime, *Jack and the Beanstalk*, in Durban, South Africa. Among the instruments he plays with "stop the show" effect is the bagpipes.

The bagpipes, we have seen, figure among the accomplishments of that great little comedian, Alec Finlay. Rikki Fulton numbers piano-playing among his resources. He can come on dressed like a concert pianist and put on a virtuoso performance on the stage grand, and I have seen him make a very good job of that old comedy stand-by which Buster Keaton resurrected in Charles Chaplin's film, *Limelight*, in which the piano comes away in the player's hands. Fulton has this sideline of the musical clown up his sleeve, and it pays a comedian to keep a few surprises for his audience.

A man whose name is on most people's lips, and whose voice is mimicked by Mike Yarwood, Peter Cavanagh and others, though his own appearances are intermittent—Chic Murray—began in a comedy musical double act with his wife, Maidie. There was some initial comedy in their contrast in sizes, she small and he tall, and he mimed amusingly as he sang to her accordion accompaniment. He also accompanies himself on the electric organ, and is a hearty yodeller.

But it was the originality of his inconsequential patter delivered in good English with a fruity Clydeside diction and intonation which took the trick with his audiences in the small halls and later in the big theatres. Chic's attack on a funny story is different from that of the average comic who gets swiftly to the pay-off line. He tells his tale in character and gets laughs all the way along in the build-up. His gesturing and his pensive expression are likewise amusing, as is his frequent silly laugh at his own idiocy. Again it is a matter of timing, and ability to sense the mood of the audience. He is at his best with an audience whose response he can feel immediately.

Characteristic of Chic Murray is the story beginning: "As I walked out of the stage door this afternoon I turned left. I usually turn right but this time I turned left: it's the spirit of adventure. I walked across the street: it was the only way I could get to the other side, and a fellow says to me: 'Is that you?' I couldn't very well deny it and me standing there ... " He sees this man jumping up and down, clapping his hands together, and Chic goes through the ridiculous motions to make it all clear to the audience, who are by this time already helpless with laughter and prepared to accept anything. The outcome of the involved yarn is that the man is trying to catch "Genumfs" and when Chic asks him what "Genumfs" are, the man replies: "I don't know: I haven't caught any yet."

His style of patter along with his accent and voice has become part of the repertoire of all the mimics. When Ronnie Barker played the Scotch engineer in *The Navy Lark* he reproduced Chic Murray's manner and diction so well that the BBC had to announce that Chic Murray was not in fact in the cast.

Talent spotters soon switched him from the smaller theatres to the larger ones before variety started to go underground. Now he appears from time to time on TV and has radio series as well as club and other engagements which take him far away from the hotel he owns in a parkside suburb of Edinburgh. He is in the film—and also now in the radio version —of *The Navy Lark*, and in other screen comedies.

Before TV curtailed a lot of theatrical activity, there was an effort at a Scottish Crazy Gang at Edinburgh Empire. Will Starr, the accordionist, was featured in the musical items which took a decidedly comic twist. A good deal of the humour was devised and presented by a versatile instrumentalist calling himself Alex Don. He was a Dalkeith man, in the fruit and vegetable business, before he took to the stage at the end of the forties. His real name is McKillop, but after running a local band, he joined Douglas, Dex, and Dale, and adopted the name Don to fit in with the alliteration. Playing about ten instruments—sax, violin, and reed and string instruments generally—he was on contract to Tom Arnold as a comic after touring with Robert Wilson in the North of Scotland, on one-night stands. He had London engagements and was in a resident show at Blackpool.

The concert tours idea comes round again and again. Especially in places where TV reception is not too good, live shows on the road are still acceptable. The late Dan Campbell, who was manager of the Palladium in East Fountainbridge, Edinburgh, when it was the home of the Lex McLean, Johnny Victory and Billy Rusk shows, had a lot of experience of touring shows before he settled down in that old Cook's Circus venue. Dan was a baritone who made some of the earliest electrical recordings for the Beltona Company. He was famous for his rendering of that stirring French war song so often featured in vaudeville programmes in Britain as well as in France. Dan used to sing it in a kilt—with a blood-stained handkerchief bound round his forehead. He recorded also *Scots Wha Hae*, *The Skye Boat Song*, *Sound the Pibroch* and *The Battle of Stirling Brig*.

As an example of what Scots entertainers were doing in the twenties, Dan was singing in the London suburban theatres—South London, Watford, Chiswick, Shepherd's Bush and Penge. He toured Moss' Empires with George West's Glasgow company. In the thirties, Dan took his own concert party to the Highlands. He carried about a dozen curtains and surrounds for three-day stands from Keith to Scrabster, Kirkwall, Lerwick, Stornoway, Portree and Oban.

At one stage in his tours, he was entertaining the divers who were engaged in bringing up the German Fleet which had been scuttled in Scapa Flow at the end of the Great War. In this job he was given the use of a boat. Once they ran into a high wind. The long scenic flats which he used in his show were blown up into the air and dived into the sea. They had to be fished out with boat hooks.

Dan drifted into singing, and into entertaining, while in the Glasgow Highlanders (the 9th—kilted—battalion of the old Highland Light Infantry). He had no training, but his comrades liked his voice and he started singing comic songs with great success. After the Great War he turned from comedy to serious singing, went in for training, and became a full-time professional before settling down in theatre management.

Music and comedy go together, and sometimes entertainers whose staple talent is singing, of various levels of seriousness, find themselves becoming typed almost as comics. Two such different singers as Moira Anderson and Lulu have introduced gags and crosstalk into their act. Kenneth McKellar has developed a good comedy line on TV along with straight actor Roddy MacMillan, and generally he is ready to use comedy in the presentation of his singing act.

Musical comics, whose act is usually very portable, fit in with the modern outlet of cabaret and club work. Frater and Gunn, a kilted double act which tours Scotland, also travel to engagements in Turkey, Greece, France, Australia, Germany, Australia, Canada, Spain and Ireland. They sing and play guitar, sax and other string and reed instruments, and they introduce some of the old traditional art of the musical clown.

A musical man who discovered a light comedy talent quite accidentally was George Elrick, who now acts as agent for some prominent Scottish entertainers, including Lena Martell. George is a "Fittie Loon," from Footdee, the fishing village which became part of the city of Aberdeen. He was originally intending to study medicine, but economic pressure owing to his father's absence on service in the hostilities of 1914-18 forced him to become a professional dance-band man. When he sang the vocals, he would smile if the lyric justified it, and the smile was conveyed in his voice. When his dance-band came on to the new booming wireless, he became known as "The Smiling Voice of Radio." It was not a publicity gimmick someone clever had thought up, but something he was told in letters from fans all over Britain. One old lady sent him a carnation every Friday. Evidently thousands of people had just been waiting to hear, drifting into their homes, a voice with a smile in it.

George is not the only entertainer who has been surprised—agreeably— by the reactions of his audience to something he just did naturally.

10

Comics
as Showmen

SCOTLAND has never had anything quite like the American burlesque
show. Certainly not the nudes or the strippers as background to the
comic. There was once a nude late-night revue in the Palladium during a
Festival (anything can happen on the Festival Fringe in Edinburgh),
and Lex McLean, whose show was on in the earlier part of the evening,
made his audience laugh by cracking: "I canna wait for ye to get my
jokes—we've to get aff for the scuddies." *Scuddie-nakit* is an old Scots
expression for *stark naked*, and so nudes, in Scots, become *scuddies*.
They never had much of a career north of the Border. Nudes may have
helped to close down English variety, but on our side it was TV and
bingo.

However, there is some approach to burlesque in the non-stop variety
or rough-hewn revue in which the comedian is the lynch-pin, and in which
he is supported by a variety of feeds, musical acts, the usual vaudeville
novelties overflowing from the circus, and, of course, girls—with clothes
on, even if it be as little as possible. The comedian may skate on thin
ice with some of his humour, but the really deep indigo material is left
to the clubs and pubs.

A number of our comedians have developed as first-class showmen,

86

not only spearheading these shows, but often promoting and guiding them, choosing the supporting acts and collaborating with their producers in the actual presentation. The show usually takes the form of a musical opening with everybody on except the comic, who breezes in after this build-up and is left in front of the curtain to make the audience laugh and put them in a mood for the rest of the show, which will include a number of situation-comedy music-hall sketches featuring the comedian and his feeds, some dance numbers by the song-and-dance man and the girls, the vaudeville acts, with vocalists much to the fore nowadays, and some more stand-up comedy from the star. There is a grand finale in panto style with the comic having the last word.

Many of the comedians I have already mentioned have been successful showmen in this genre—Sir Harry Lauder himself, who was early in on the concert parties with the violinist Mackenzie Murdoch; Harry Gordon, Alec Finlay, and Andy Stewart, in particular. The home of this kind of show is Glasgow Pavilion, with its seaside rivals—particularly Ayr Gaiety under the Popplewells, in which most of the good comics had their training, not only in putting across their individual humour but in troupe work.

Much missed in this scene is Tommy Morgan, the big "ba'-faced" comic with the gravel voice whose mother's ejaculation—"Aw, Clairty, Clairty!", a corruption of "I declare to God"—became his catch-phrase and his nickname to the working million of Clydeside and the Industrial Belt. He was a real East End Glasgow boy and a natural exponent of Glasgow working-class humour, to which all the ordinary folk of Scotland respond and which gives a good laugh to the upper echelons as well. Whether one laughed *with* Tommy, or *at* him, he achieved his object of keeping everybody in a good mood till the end of the show and beyond.

After well over a dozen successive seasons at the Metropole, Stockwell Street (the former Scotia Music-Hall), in panto, Tommy put on his own summer shows in the Pavilion, and these ran for a score of years and became a Glasgow institution. I saw him first as a pierrot at Portobello and found him irresistibly funny with the poorest of material. He was the type of which it could be said: "It's no' what he says; it's the wey he says it."

With his round haggis face glowing and always seeming on the point of bursting, he was just like an overgrown schoolboy dying to tell you of the latest lark, and the general impact was what Glasgow folk call "a rerr terr at the Ferr" (a rare tear at the Fair).

If Tommy Yorke was telling him a story about something that happened away over in South America on the Pampas, Tommy could paralyse everybody just by repeating "The Pampas!" with extra explosive force, spraying the straight man in his enthusiasm. He was the Scottish type whom Robert Burns and Sir Walter Scott would have described as "an honest chiel." He would have been perfect in the role of Tam o' Shanter. I can remember little of what he ever said—only that he made me laugh, and thousands with me.

In the tradition as comic and star of a show, with all the thrills of old variety, are Johnny Beattie and Jack Milroy, both men who have benefited from the enterprise of the Popplewells at Ayr Gaiety. Johnny Beattie, an ex-Royal Marine, is billed as Scotland's sophisticated comedy star.'. His appearance and manner of putting over his rapid-fire succession of quips have acquired an air of sophistication, but the accent is still delight-fully Scottish, and the background from which he draws much of his humour is industrial Scotland.

Two of his cracks recently struck me as clever. One, in autobiographical mood: "I'm really half Irish. My mother always said I was half Irish and half daft." The other, at a TV Hogmanay party at which he was the host (STV, with Helen McArthur, Calum Kennedy and the Alexander Brothers): "It's no' that I like drinking, but it passes the time till ye're fou."

Johnny Beattie was Wishee Washee to Duncan Macrae's Widow Twankey in Alhambra panto (*Aladdin*) and has retained a great admiration for "Big John" (Macrae's full Christian names were John Duncan) as a performer and a person. Last Christmas and New Year (1972-73) Beattie was the star of the original Ayr Gaiety panto, *Up the Beanstalk*, which ran into March, and his summer seasons also are long-running. He is a wholehearted student of show business—particularly admires Bing Crosby and Schnozzle Durante—and really throws himself into these lively entertainments.

King of the comic showmen in Scotland is Lex McLean, whose transfer to TV was reluctant but successful. He really was a music-hall man and has always enjoyed his audience as much as his audience enjoyed him. To see him on TV is to glimpse only a fleeting shadow of what Lex was like playing up a Glasgow Pavilion or Edinburgh Palladium audience, from the moment he dismissed the dancing girls and came out front-curtain to say: "Aw right, now ye can get tore into your caramels. Dinna pey any attention to me, just carry on chatting among yersels!" I have never known a comedian with such a constant flow of chatter, good, bad, and indifferent, but always, because of Lex's personality, laugh-making.

Una McLean, a vivacious "gallus lass," lends her warm-hearted cheer to *Melody Inn*, a costumed revival of "pub music-hall" with anachronistic hand-mikes on Grampian TV.

Andy Stewart stepped jauntily from a supporting role in a Bridie play to his own show business in the Lauder comedy and song tradition.

Sex in the Supermarket. Rik[ ]
Fulton (left) as the garrulou[s]
"Josie" and Jack Milroy (righ[t])
as the automatically amorou[s]
"Francie" in typical situatio[n]
comedy.

A "Teuchter" show: a tartan-cla[d]
group of varied types of enter[ ]
tainers: Alec Finlay and th[e]
Royal Clansmen on Grampia[n]
TV.

To me, since Tommy Lorne, he has been the funniest man on the Scottish stage. His TV series, according to Mr Iain MacFadyen, the senior light entertainment producer for Scotland on the BBC, pulled in a million viewers. In 1971 Lex had a serious brain operation, but before long he was back on TV and back in his favourite medium, the live performance with an audience that has paid to hear him. More recently he collapsed in the middle of one of his amusing routines in a Glasgow bingo hall. He blamed the overheating of the premises in which the performance took place. This meant a further curtailment of his engagements, in which he always gives wholeheartedly "of his best." He has performed in English clubs with success, for, although Lex can talk thickly Scotch with his own home audience, he can be highly adaptable and is funny even if you don't get all that he says. Also he is an ever-ready musician.

Lex, who resides in Helensburgh with his wife of twenty years—his blonde, charming and infinitely understanding, "amazing Grace"—got some of his training at the seaside with the Popplewells of Ayr and was in their 1931 *Whirl of Gaiety*. He was as popular in Edinburgh as in Glasgow, breaking all records for theatre attendances in the capital, and in 1957 his show ran during the Festival. That was when I called him "King of the Festival Fringe." The Fringe turned up trumps for some visiting quickfiremen—notably the *Beyond the Fringe* quartet—but none of them could make an Edinburgh audience laugh as much as McLean did. Before him at Fringe time the Palladium had gone over to straight drama, with casts headed by Duncan Macrae or Sonia Dresdel, followed by late-night revues of the highbrow Oxford and Cambridge type. Lex could stand up to all that. He played to capacity houses all through the Festival, proving that what the majority of the people wanted was not education or uplift but a good laugh. His show consisted of healthy vaudeville, a refined chorus, jazz singers, and Lex, Lex and more Lex.

McLean is a handsome, dark-featured Clydeside Gael who could pass for an Italian with his long nose and his flashing smile. Now in his early sixties, he looks back to a most varied career. He was apprenticed to the shipyards but decided he did not want to build giant Cunarders or even wee boats. He confesses he was bored by riveting, and kept his eye on the clock for breaking-up time, or, as we Scots call it, "lowzin' time."

Instead he became a pianist and it was in that capacity that he toured England with the Royal Scottish Kilt Show. To vary his musical act he became straight man to several comics in succession, notably to George West, the panto and summer season star of the thirties and forties. He played the accordion, the clarinet, and the saxophone.

It dawned on him eventually that he was not really a straight man, and could be at least as funny as the men he fed. He still turns to music as relief from his fun, and is capable of bringing tears to the audience's eyes with his renderings of popular numbers in the midst of the general hilarity. Undoubtedly the stuff of which music-hall was made in the old days, and if variety ever comes back it will need characters like Lex McLean to restore it.

As a comedian, Lex has often been regarded as "blue-nosed." In the days when the Lord Chamberlain's office was still reading the scripts of music-hall acts along with straight drama, and entertainers could be fined for introducing doubtful material unpassed by the censor, Lex delighted in blinding the Lord Chamberlain with science. His scripts were impeccable, but seeing them performed in the theatre was another matter. I have seen Lex win his biggest laughs by giving the good lines to his feeds, while all he did was look the audience "straight in the eye" as if to ask: "What do you make of that?" And the audience usually made the most of it. Indeed, Lex could easily have pleaded that it was his audience that was being dirty: and he could be right.

A typical sketch was the one in which he played a Dame part as the woman who had written to the Lonely Hearts Club and expected a visit from a male heart-throb as a consequence. The lines became crossed, and her visitor was a man who wanted to demonstrate a vacuum cleaner. He did not have the apparatus with him but proceeded to tell her what he intended doing. Lex, as the woman, did little in this sketch except make faces or adopt attitudes of shock which suggested consistent mis-interpretation of what the man was saying. It was the kind of sketch of which you could say: "Not a word out of place." Only the thoughts of the audience went astray, assisted by Lex's baffled expression. One of his tricks is to mime expressions of amazement and mouth words which challenge the audience's skill at suspicious lip-reading. His piercing dark eyes reach right into the murky recesses of the populace's mind. He is no more blue than his audience. Strangely, there are bus loads of respectable middle-aged housewives to hear him.

Dame acts are thrown in by Lex as part of his wide-ranging menu. He used to do one solo, standing up as an unmarried lady, "not entirely neglected," as the old music-hall saying went, and telling story after story of adventures with designing males. There was the one who took her into the cemetery, and she still had the impression on her back: "Sacred to the Memory of Paddy Reilly." This act concluded with a spirited rendering of:

> "Oh dear me, what will I dae
> If I dee an auld maid in a garret?"

He threw in a few old-man parts as well, in one, as a shepherd, bringing on his own dog, and wearing thick pebble glasses which gave him an eery, elfin look. He would crack the joke: "In the Boer War they put something in our tea to keep us frae chasing the Zulu women. I think it's beginning to work."

Scotch comedians as a whole keep up the Lauder tradition of being relatively clean. But with an artist like McLean it is a case of knowing his audience and just how far he can go with them. He is like Max Miller, the Cheeky Chappie. Lex's cheek was based on a sound knowledge of his Pavilion and Palladium audiences. Lex is a master of *double entendre*, and has permitted the circulation of his nickname, "Sexy Lexie," and yet there is nothing really vicious in his humour.

It is the humour of release, to which a pent-up audience suffering from all the stresses of the social system immediately responds. And a lot of the effect is due to the hypermanic manner of his delivery. The stuff just bubbles out of him, as from a talkative man in a pub. Out it pours—puns, cracks about topical events, fragments of folk rhyme, asides to the audience about other artists on the bill, funny stories (never too long or involved and with the pay-off line perfectly timed), ad libs about people coming in late or going out in the middle of the act, and silences punctuated by looks which speak more than words. His sketches range over the commonplaces of working-class life—rows with the wife and the mother-in-law or with the younger generation, "burroo" situations (the old employment exchange or modern social security, with Lex as the persistent workshy and malingerer), what the English North Country comedians call "flat-cap comedy," Andy Capp stuff. Or he is a WRAC girl with other drag comics in an outrageous take-off of the "all girls together" business, where again the cracks are "just how you take them."

His Pavilion and Palladium shows were carried on at such a high pitch that when I went to talk to him in his dressing-room afterwards he seemed not only relaxed but depressed, as if he had emptied all the fun out of himself and poured it into the audience. As they left the theatre smiling, Lex sat glum, looking like Joe Grimaldi—"yours truly, Grim All Day." That flashing show of teeth had been entirely transferred from his own face to the faces of the customers, and he seemed to suffer a sort of hang-over. One time I stood in the wings and he came off drenched with sweat. "There must be easier ways of making a living," he remarked to me.

Youngsters with stage ambitions learn a lot if they hitch their wagons to such stars. Billy Rusk and Johnny Victory were two other comedians whose shows helped young artists in their stage careers—tap dancers, singers, instrumentalists: such shows, though centred on the comics, promote other types of acts, and the performers gain experience by participating as supports in the sketches as well as in the ensembles.

The late Johnny Victory was an admirer of Sir Harry Lauder and ran an old car of Sir Harry's, but his act was nothing like the Lauder type. His individual contributions were monologues, and a "Maurice Chevalier" *cum* "Jean Sablon" French turn. He was one of the few Scotch comics to emerge from Edinburgh. His father was a local business man, Peter Victory, who transferred from selling fish to running taxis. Johnny Victory used to crack: "Now they tell me that as a comic I'm a good taxi-driver wasted."

He was not in the Lex McLean class as a comedian, though he presented the same shape of show. Johnny, in comparison, "joked wi' deeficulty." His humour was on the heavy side and, while you could say he was a tolerable performer, he could not keep his audience in a state of hilarity as McLean did. Lex's technique of getting them laughing with quick-fire gags, until they are amused at complete nonsense and non-sequiturs, was beyond Victory. But he also was a big help to young artists climbing up through the halls. Roy Castle remembered him with gratitude, and the young crooner, Jackie Dennis, got his second wind in the Victory show.

Scottish Television built Larry Marshall up into a leading comic. Larry, a sympathetic Scots-Italian originally surnamed Tomasso, handled audience participation programmes with skill and acceptability in the early days of commercial TV and led a group of vaudeville artists in the *One O'Clock Gang*. He has had a career as a comic since then, in pantomime in Glasgow and Edinburgh, and was host at Scottish Television's Burns Supper in January 1973. His most ambitious show venture was a one-man effort at the Palladium on the Festival Fringe, with the help of the TV producer, Liam Hood. The best thing in it was Larry as a "poison dwarf," as a German restaurateur designated our Glasgow soldiery. This anticipated to some extend W. Gordon Smith's one-man show, *Jock*, written for, and performed by Russell Hunter, in the Festival Fringe of 1972.

There has been a vogue of one-man entertainments on the Fringe since Larry Marshall, and I wonder if he gets credit for being a pioneer. The others have been more on the "straight comedy" side, but they are obviously related as an art form. In February 1973 Larry, as chairman of the Stars for Spastics in Scotland, presided at a dinner for four hundred to mark the finals of the elbow-wrestling championships. He was featured in the King's, Glasgow, pantomime, *Aladdin*, that winter. More recently he has headed the variety bill in an Edinburgh hotel cabaret.

TV and radio to a certain degree have kept up the tradition of the variety show spearheaded by the comic, as in the case of Larry Marshall. The present-day equivalent is *Alec Finlay and the Royal Clansmen* and Andy Stewart in *Scotch Corner*. Una McLean, Ron Dale and Danny Street in *Melody Inn*, another Grampian Television presentation, carry on the tradition of reviving the atmosphere of the music-hall in the days when it was a "happening" in a pub.

On radio there is almost a revival of the seaside, pierrot type of programme, with a string of turns introduced by a comic compere. Jack Radcliffe starred in some of these not long before his death. Recently Glen Michael has proved his skill as a rapid-fire gagster in introducing acts in such productions, both seaside radio and programmes with Brian Fahey and the new Scottish Radio Orchestra. Johnny Beattie also has been a success in compering the "big band" revivals of Fahey. Our modern Scotch comics work easily in the George Jessel, Milton Berle, Al Burnett compere tradition. Yet they remain very Scotch.

11

Born in
a Trunk

A TRUE son of the old Music-hall is Jimmy Logan, though he is still in his mid forties. His father and mother, Jack Short and May Dalziel, were a double act over forty years ago. Jimmy's aunt, Ella Logan, was a famous Broadway jazz singer, and the family adopted her name for stage purposes.

The Logan Family started to appear at the Metropole in Stockwell Street—originally the Scotia, Glasgow's oldest music hall—in the thirties, and in 1943 Jack Short took over production there. In 1947 he started the Logan Family shows, which rapidly established themselves as part of Glasgow's way of life.

On leaving school at 15, Jimmy plunged into the hereditary business as a singer and instrumentalist. Before he was 16, it was recognised that he was a born comedian and he became not only an essential part of the family act but the comedy lead in their summer show at the Metropole. His sister became famous as the jazz singer, Annie Ross.

After the war he became one of the standbys of the Glasgow and Edinburgh panto and summer show trade. He developed his own line of humour as a cheeky Glasgow boy and has played in many a panto classroom riot as "silly Jimmy Logan." Tommy Lorne used to say he was passionately fond of a couple of sausages for his breakfast, and Jimmy publicly confessed to a similar predilection with his catch phrase: "Sausages is the boys." Another of his catch phrases was "Smashin', in't it?" in that long-drawn Glasgow drawl—"Smaaashin'!" It became a household word in Scotland, far beyond the Glasgow city bounds.

When the film of *Floodtide* on a Clydeside industrial theme was made with Gordon Jackson, Elizabeth Sellars and Rona Anderson as the romantic triangle, Jimmy Logan appeared in it with Janet Brown as the lighter relief, and he was perfectly cast as the slim and cool young Glaswegian with his ballroom patter: "Smashin' flerr, in't it? D'ye come here often?" and his act at the piano with the Rutherglen comedienne brought the real atmosphere of the region on to the screen. Now he is in *Carry On Abroad* and fits in easily with the well-known team of English comics in that successful series. He appeared also in the film, *The Wild Affair*, with Nancy Kwan.

In March 1973 he embarked on still another new departure, taking over from Terry Scott in the comedy hit, *The Mating Game*, at the Apollo Theatre, London, with Aimi MacDonald and Julia Lockwood. This was his first acting role in the West End, though he has played London before. He was in one London Palladium panto (1968) with Engelbert Humperdinck, and as long ago as 1954 he was on the programme in that theatre with Johnnie Ray. In the winter of 1972-73 he was Buttons in *Cinderella* at Edinburgh King's and in Christmas-New Year 1973-74 he is back in the same panto in his native Glasgow. In both summer shows and panto he has shown his great versatility.

He vies with Stanley Baxter in his talent for mimicry, and in one Hogmanay show on TV he did a great Nina and Frederick act. He is strong on the character side as a gamekeeper or a Highland athlete, and in contrast to that he has appeared devastatingly in "drag" as a Mistinguett-type *Mademoiselle de Paris*. I doubt if there is anything Jimmy can't do in the comedy line, and he is ideal for cabaret as a singing pianist with an original line in comic song and parody, with a flair for topical reference. He is delighted to show that he is no hidebound Glasgow "hooker-doon" comic but can produce the sophisticated stuff.

He is an artist who gives a good deal of study to his performances. The Metropole was a hard school, where the audience soon let you know if your act was not up to standard.

I saw Jimmy in yet another light almost a score of years ago, when he was still a lad in his mid twenties. I looked in at a meeting of the Scottish section of the British Actors Equity Association in an Edinburgh hotel lounge. Jimmy was still the natural comic. That side of his nature is irrepressible. Scoring wisecracks off well-known theatrical colleagues, slipping hotel ashtrays into his pocket, he was much the young man with whom I did a radio show early in his career in Glasgow. But even then, though he was still very much a boy bubbling over with fun, he showed his serious side. He was there to plead the cause of the chorus girl in the less remunerative type of show. His audience was composed of people whose lives were remote from those of the chorus girl, though they belonged in a wide sense to the same profession. Most of the people listening were actors and actresses associated with repertory, and so-called "legitimate" theatre or "straight" drama.

Duncan Macrae was in the chair of the meeting, wearing a beard he had grown for the part of the warlock in Alexander Reid's comedy, *The Warld's Wonder*, and addressing the assembly in the meticulous English of a Scottish schoolmaster. On his left sat Lennox Milne, the actress and producer wife of the late Moray MacLaren, who was a grand Scottish writer. Another prominent Scottish actress, Madeleine Christie, was there, too.

The Scottish section, Duncan explained, was "a modest little committee, in full communion with the British Actors Equity Association." On his right sat the Scottish organiser, Alec McCrindle, who had recently returned to his homeland after twenty years on the London stage and on films, and who has since been active in TV. As Scottish organiser, McCrindle, then based at Kippen, Stirling, toured the Scottish theatres, calling on members and managements, in ice shows, straight plays, non-stop variety programmes with weekly changes of programme, BBC studios, wherever Equity members were playing and there were differences to be ironed out. He told me: "At our committee meetings the hundreds-of-pounds-a-week men sit with the five-pounds-a-week girls." (These were rates in 1954.)

Introducing Jimmy Logan, Duncan Macrae (who looked like Uncle Sam in his goatee beard, horn-rimmed glasses and slanting left forelock) called the younger comedian "a man who doesn't need to try very hard to earn his four pund ten a week."

Jimmy did not dramatise or exaggerate his appeal for fair conditions for the girls of the chorus in the Number Two theatres. He stated simply, in his caressing Glasgow accent, that Equity were out for a negotiated contract for artists which would ensure a reasonable minimum salary for choristers. He gave his experience negotiating with managements on the chorus girls' behalf, and again there was no exaggeration, no dramatics.

Moderately he stated that at times managements were not easy people to negotiate with. He warmed up as he attacked a rival association's contract and moved on to an eloquent appeal for a strong Equity, and a seven-pounds minimum wage for chorus girls. (The average wage of women in industry at that time had risen to £5 12s 8d a week.)

Bad times for theatre people naturally loomed up in the discussion in that Princes Street hotel that day, for 1955 was a watershed. Theatres in Scotland had been closing down. Ayr Gaiety had not long before been burnt down, but McCrindle was able that day to report that the Jack Milroy show from Ayr had been successfully transferred to Leith Gaiety, another variety theatre which had closed down, not long before that, for lack of public support.

TV, they were saying in 1955, was the scourge of variety as a whole, but there were still audiences then for good variety presented by Lex McLean, Johnny Victory, Denny Willis, Jack Milroy, and a few others.

Actor-manager Wilson ("Bill") Barrett had just abandoned his three-cities (Glasgow, Edinburgh, Aberdeen) repertory enterprise because of the impact of TV. "The theatre will go through a perilous couple of years before it comes back into its own again," Bill told me. Occasional films on Scottish themes were giving temporary work to Scottish artists.

This Equity meeting, with Scottish players—straight and comic—discussing their conditions, gave me a new slant on the theatre, and yet another interesting facet of the multiple personality of Jimmy Logan. Since then he has made valiant efforts to keep live theatre in existence in Glasgow, with his New Metropole venture which continued into 1972, and which he has not yet completely given up. Besides being a highly entertaining comic, Jimmy has been a tower of strength to theatre in Scotland.

12

Women's Ad-lib

SCOTSMEN are not as a rule very keen on women as comics. They prefer men dressed up as Dames giving full rein to a masculine satire of femininity rough and smooth. Yet there have been some very successful comediennes on the Scottish stage and some who have plunged whole-heartedly into the portrayal of back-green, stairhead, wash-house, and kitchen-sink harridans—the sort of part which might be thought safer in the hands of robust male clowns of the Arthur Lucan type.

Long before Stanley Baxter discovered the humorous potential of the Glasgow dialect (Glescaranto) studied as a foreign language, with translations into high-falutin' English to accentuate the comedy, a music-hall double act, Lindsay and Harte, were scoring heavily with this juxtaposition of street talk and drawing-room elocution. They specialised in Glasgow characters, but their act was very popular outside of Glasgow, and they were well known at Edinburgh Theatre Royal and Leith Alhambra.

Dora Lindsay and Bret Harte belonged to the period when revue was taking over from vaudeville. There was a spate of revues with arbitrary, and usually silly, titles leading up to the Great War and continuing through to the twenties. I find that Lindsay and Harte were topping the variety bill at Leith Alhambra in 1915 with an act based on Barrowland, a kind of Glasgow version of Petticoat Lane. They came back again and again in a series of "All-Scotch Revues." A typical title was *It's a Nice Day*, one of Dora Lindsay's catch phrases, like Harry Gordon's "It's been an awfu' day o' midges."

Dora was a wee woman with a complete mastery of the intricacies and nuances of Glasgow working-class speech. Her partner Bret Harte was tall, and a most accomplished comedian and feed, clever at the slow burn and the double take and "Come again!"—those tricks and expressions with which character comedians punctuate the absurdity of the situation. Sometimes he was in "hooker-doon" flat cap and muffler (or, as the Glaswegians call it, "gravvitt"), joining with Dora in the dialect and the "fly talk." But more often than not he was the better-dressed, upstage type, looking down his nose at the wee Glasgow woman and professing to be baffled by her "Macfarlane."

In their best sketches, this contrast was played to the full. Dora was the wee shawlie, or "herrie" (a woman with her hair uncovered, without a hat), with or without her teeth in, coming out every now and then with a mouthful of rhyming slang or with the unadulterated speech of St Mungo. Bret was the would-be Kelvinsider, the pretended representative of "only those and such as those," who considered he would be letting himself down socially if he gave any inkling that he knew what she meant. It might be caricature, but it was not too far-fetched a travesty of a real-life situation. The Kelvinsider's pretence not to understand the talk of the Gallowgate is a commonplace attitude, paralleled in many places besides Glasgow.

A Lindsay and Harte masterpiece was the revue *Bachles*, taking its title from the Glasgow word for old, dilapidated shoes. It was repeated in several versions, for the Lindsay and Harte scripts, if they ever existed non-orally, were free and easy and depended on audience reaction and spur-of-the-moment decisions. It had a plot of a kind, something to do with a precious stone stolen by a gang and hidden in the heel of a cast-off shoe.

What I remember most, of this revue of almost half a century ago, is of Lindsay and Harte in a scene in a posh shoe shop, in which Harte was the immaculate shop-walker speaking with "a bool in his mooth" over a choker collar, and Dora was the wee shawlie with a snivelling "wean" in tow.

"Seeza perra bits fur meena wain!" said Dora, and Bret's face expressed his bewilderment. He tried to break the sentence down into its components in order to grasp its significance. "Seize?" he echoed, gesturing appropriately. "Naw," said Dora, "seeza perra bits fur meena wain!" Even when it was sorted out that "Seez" meant "Give me!" there was still the problem of how he could supply one pair of boots for her and the child. I am sure Lindsay and Harte had actually heard some Glasgow woman give such an order in a shoe shop. It had the stamp of authenticity, even if they carried it on to wring the last gasp of laughter from the audience.

It was still a time when the comic song was a strong ingredient of variety, revue, and pantomime. Almost every comedian or comedienne had a song regarded as more or less exclusive, or at least suited to the stage personality. Songs lasted a long time in their popularity. They would be plugged at seaside resorts in the summer-time, sometimes by pavement concert parties promoting the wares of song publishers and selling sheet music, and they would still be ringing in our ears all through panto time, and if they were particularly good they would be back on the beaches and sandy sidewalks the following summer. We bought the song sheets, and those of us who could, pounded the jingly-jangly tunes out on the piano. There were more pianos around then, and there was more singing in our homes.

Two of Dora Lindsay's songs that come back to me fragmentarily are "I'm not a can—I'm Dorothy Ann," and "Ruglen's wee roon rid lums reek briskly." I cannot remember more than the refrain phrases, but I still have a picture of Dora and hear her "belting it out." She held us in the hollow of her hand. Eventually she left us for Australia, where she found a new appreciative audience.

A later feminine expert at the "close-mooth" type of Glasgow comedy was Doris Droy, a double act with her musician husband Frank, and also a participant in sketches with the celebrated Queen's panto comic, Sam Murray. Doris was good at the kind of slanging match that arises between women hanging out the washing in a city back court—the mutual recriminations bringing in all the skeletons from the family cupboards: "Yer man's a deserter!" was one of her war-time phrases, in a period when indeed many men of military age had gone underground in a city where it was easy to disappear, and even to live without an identity or a ration card. There was always a streak of grim realism about the comedy at the Queen's Theatre.

It was the kind of place where the comics would do a tap dance in big boots without socks and with the laces untied, and play the spoons down their trouser legs like street-corner buskers. The Queen's pantos were great favourites with Kelvinsiders "going slumming," and the humour could be outrageous. Doris Droy, a refined lady offstage, took it all in her stride.

Doris Droy is an example of the comic who started as a singer. She was gifted with a melodious voice which continued to give pleasure to her audiences long after her Glasgow theatre had closed down and she had turned to entertaining in the clubs and pubs of the North of England. She was a people's artist from the first. As a teenager she went in for go-as-you-please competitions at the seaside—"doon the watter" at Dunoon—and she had quite a career at such resorts as Rothesay and Troon before she made Glasgow.

It was when she was entertaining on the beach at Troon as a member of the Royal Caledonian pierrots that she was asked to do a broad Glasgow dialect part, and she switched with ease from her refined Scots-English to Glescaranto, which always appealed to the Fair holidaymakers on Clydeside. Like Renee Houston, she tried her hand at a sister act and for some time worked under the promotion of the magician Bodie. Eventually she teamed up with Frank Droy.

She also was a comedienne who had an immediate *rapport* with her audience. She knew what they were thinking, and helped them to think it. She sailed easily through her act, tacking and veering to suit the mood of the gallery. Just a natural comic, and never very straitlaced about it. She became known as "Suicide Sal," and her comic songs and jokes were always popular.

When the theatre world started to contract in Glasgow, Frank and Doris Droy took their double act to England and worked the clubs, especially in the North, where Scots artists are fairly well understood. They had a fresh and successful career until Doris's death, after which Frank played the piano for a while at the Star and Garter Hotel in Leeds. He died in the Yorkshire city while this book was in preparation. Another couple of good old troupers gone!

Another comedienne in the broadest Scots was Jean Kennedy, who had a bold line in humour.

An old-time comedienne still going strong on the boards—she was one of Johnny Beattie's guests in his show at Glasgow Pavilion in the spring of 1973—is Gracie Clark, again the strong partner in a famous double act—Clark and Murray, entertainers at the piano. Gracie has been popular in seaside and city shows for more years than she might care to tell, and her songs and patter, with her husband as pianist and stooge, can still hit the high spots of entertainment.

Her asides to the audience about her husband—"the wee sowl"—are famous, and have equal appeal to the men and women in the audience.

She is the taller of the two—a situation which is always regarded as comical. The typically Glaswegian humour of the "stories from the police courts" in the Scottish paper, *Weekly News*, makes great play of the "Big Aggie and Wee Shooie" complex. Gracie's warm, patronising attitude to her partner gives the joke a richer bouquet.

Probably the most talented comedienne Scotland ever produced has been Renee Houston, still very much to the fore on radio in *Petticoat Line*. She has had so many distinctive and successful careers that she would make a study in herself, but we in Scotland remember affectionately her double acts, first with her sister Billie (The Houston Sisters) and later with her husband Donald Stewart. I see from the books of La Scala Electric Theatre, Edinburgh, that the Houston Sisters were there in 1924 playing for £16 between them. That was in the days when turns alternated with two-reeler films on the cinema circuits. £16 was considered "going places."

The Houstons were of theatrical stock, daughters of James and Elizabeth Gribben, Houston being their mother's maiden name. Renee was born in Johnstone, Renfrewshire, in 1902, and was barely 14 and still at school when she made her first stage appearance. She started appearing in concerts and then teamed with her sister Billie in their famous act. Two years after that La Scala date they were in the Royal Variety Performance and by the thirties they were touring France and Switzerland as well as appearing frequently in the glittering variety programmes in London's West End.

One remembers Renee in those days as a curly-headed cutie scoring with rapid-fire, effervescent humour and wit over the patient Billie dressed as a boy. In a recent radio programme Renee recalled how the Houston Sisters got their big break in the South. They were at the Shoreditch Empire when the star comedian, Wilkie Bard ("I want to sing in opera"), was late. They were told to stretch out their act.

Now the great thing about Renee has always been her resourcefulness and I imagine the expertise with which she extended her turn made a deep impression on the professionals who saw her. Later she was changing into her soldier suit in the wings and asked a man standing nearby to help her. She did not know who he was, and when she asked his name, he said: "Last night my name was Wilkie Bard—now it's just Barred."

Soon she was not only appearing up West. She was even writing and producing revue for Tom Arnold, and after Billie's illness brought a halt to their double act, she was playing in musical comedy, *Love Laughs*, at London Hippodrome (1935), and in *Certainly, Sir* in 1936. Her double act with her husband brought her back to the variety circuits, including her beloved Glasgow. She was in the Royal Variety Performance again in 1938, toured South Africa, did several pantos and teamed up with Billie again in a revival of their old act, by now nostalgically remembered, at Victoria Palace in March 1950.

Renee is such a born professional, and has such a natural genius for adaptability, that there is very little of which she is incapable in the entertainment line, and it was not surprising that she was able to switch from variety acts to straight plays as well as revues and musical comedies. The talkies were another outlet for her talents, and she has made impressive appearances as a featured player in several good films, notably as one of the displaced and wandering women in the Far East in *A Town Like Alice*. She has fitted in, as the great trouper that she is, in *The Horse's Mouth* and the *Carry On* series. Her first adventure in cinema was in 1941 in *A Girl Must Live*.

In her variety act, part of Renee Houston's ability to amuse was derived from the old Glasgow linguistic contrast. She could talk awfully posh Kelvinside or Mayfair or lapse into her broader accent. She was fond of chattering in asides to the audience and to the orchestra, and she had a gift for repartee and topical reference which, to judge from her radio impromptus, has not left her. She came up through a hard school. She also has a good memory for stories and a professional skill in telling them, though she makes it sound easy, as if any of us could do the same. She is of the stuff of old music-hall and one is almost tempted to reflect "They don't make them like that any more."

Since Renee's variety days, the most distinguished individual talent to emerge among Scotswomen in the entertainment field is that of Margot Henderson, that accomplished mimic and singer at the piano. Her impersonations had a great vogue on the halls and on TV, and more recently she has been starring at *Talk of the Town* in London clubland. Her act is ideal for the intimate atmosphere of the clubs, but is welcome to a wider audience.

A bright and attractive comedienne has delighted us in the post-war years in Una McLean, star of pantomime in the Number One theatres and popular in music-hall on TV, appearing in highly acceptable series with Ron Dale and Danny Street (*Melody Inn*, Grampian), in which she shows her cheerful skill with audience participation.

One of the staunchest troupers of the variety stage has been Helen

Norman, a product of the North-East and a niece of that great vaudeville artist, the magician and hypnotist, Dr Walford Bodie. Helen was the great support of the late Jack Radcliffe and an example of the feed who can be a complete act in herself. One of the most fondly remembered appearances of Jack Radcliffe and Helen together was in a sketch in which they met as two old folk in a city park, and in the course of their casual "passing the time of day" conversation discovered they were old stage partners. They recalled their double act and proceeded to go through their routine once again, becoming transformed almost to youngsters in the process.

Another was the boy and girl sketch where Jack was a country yokel seeing a lassie home, wheeling her bike as she walked by his side. When they got to the farmhouse gate, Helen made it plain that she was responding to his advances more than somewhat. At the end she told him: "Ye can have anything frae me—anything ye want.'' Jack replied: "Oh, thanks: I'll take yer bike," grabbing it and making off as the lights went out.

Since Radcliffe's demise Helen has soldiered on and has been in demand in panto. Following her as a feminine foil of Scottish comics has been Marillyn Gray, a straight actress from Perth and its famous Repertory Theatre, who starred in plays with the Gateway Theatre Company, playing opposite Tom Fleming and other notable actors. She played the title role in Alexander Reid's period drama of the Border reivers, *The Lass wi' the Muckle Mou*, and she was Jenny Clow in a 1954 Festival production of Robert Kemp's play on Robert Burns, *T'Other Dear Charmer*, and the fair victim in James Bridie's Burke and Hare drama, *The Anatomist*, 1956. She adapted easily to acting as feed to Jimmy Logan in pantomime and summer show and seems to be as much at home among variety artists as among straight players, although there are such vast differences in technique between the two styles of presentation.

A comedienne who has scored on radio and TV is Molly Weir, whom I first heard impersonating Tommy Morgan in Carrol Levis's *Discoveries*.

Margot Henderson's effervescence as a mimic at the piano has made her act equally adaptable to stage, radio, cabaret and TV.

Showmanship is in the blood of Jimmy Logan, who grew up in his family entertainment business, but he likes to step out of traditional Scotch comedy into cabaret and straight plays on the London West End stage.

Russell Hunter, character actor
and TV success as "Lonely" in
Callan, enjoys his interludes as a
Scotch panto comedian as well as
his one-man shows on the
Edinburgh Festival Fringe.
He is depicted here in the BBC
production of *Cocky*

Molly Weir, famous as "Aggie,"
the Scotch servant lass in the
Bebe Daniels radio series, *Life
with the Lyons*, launched herself
into variety entertainment as a
young mimic of Tommy Morgan.
(Photograph, BBC.)

13

Feeds
and
Stooges

STRAIGHT men is what some feeds or stooges prefer to call themselves. Strictly speaking the stooge is he who gets slapped, and as the roles are often reversed in a double act, it is difficult sometimes to work out which is the comic and which is the stooge. The straight man is the gentleman of the act, not so comically dressed as his comedian, and in Scotland usually talking a high-falutin English in contrast to the comic's broad tongue (almost invariably Glasgow).

In many cases the feed is more a supporting comic, called upon to do a fair amount of broad comedy in sketches and in most cases able to appear in an act of his own. Such feeds tend to hive off and become comics in their own right. In pantomime the feed qualifies for one of the important comedy roles—a Bad Baron if he is the gentlemanly or heavy actor type, an Ugly Sister or one of the Robbers. The Uglies and the Robbers are double acts in themselves, and are often the roles chosen for well-known stage partners.

In the revues or non-stop variety shows which were going strong before TV knocked the music halls hard, sometimes the leading comedian peopled his stage with supporting comics. It was like the Commedia dell'Arte all over again, with the supporting comics performing the traditional comic roles—the old man, the doctor, the policeman (derived from the swaggering captain of the Renaissance comedies), the stock figures of the harlequinade, but in modern dress.

Lex McLean's Pavilion sketches used just about everybody in the show, including pop singers and dancers, and they all enjoyed their turn of being funny. In his stage presentations of the familiar kitchen-sink, working-class or unemployed family situation, he made great use of that old tried and trusty variety act—Carr and Vonnie. I first saw Carr and Vonnie singing and dancing in the old Metropole in Stockwell Street, Glasgow. They came on as a well-dressed pair of tourists. You might take them for Americans until you heard Jimmy Carr's piping Glasgow voice or Vonnie's deeper Irish, for Vonnie was a colleen who preserved her accent, though she could make Scotch noises when required.

To their singing and dancing ability, Carr and Vonnie added plenty of experience in pantomime, particularly in the Glasgow Queen's, the most Glaswegian of them all. They would be anything from the fore and hind legs of the horse (which danced of course) to the supports in a fully cast knockabout sketch. Lex's Pavilion and Palladium sketches used Vonnie as the scolding wife, and Carr frequently as the small boy of the family. These are true professionals, all-rounders, able to turn on their own singing and dancing act, and also to fit into all the requirements of the general conspiracy to raise a laugh.

In TV, another Carr, Walter, as already mentioned, has been Lex's main feed. Walter achieved fame as a comedy actor in the fifties. His weak-kneed servant in *The Flouers o Edinburgh* (1954-55), by Robert McLellan, was conspicuous enough to be caricatured by Ronald Searle in *Punch*. He presented a lugubrious, dilapidated, knock-kneed, shuffling figure, in a turban copied from the statue of the eighteenth century poet, Allan Ramsay, at the Floral Clock in Princes Street.

He was an actor brilliant enough to succeed Duncan Macrae in the Festival production of Robert Kemp's *Let Wives Tak Tent* (from Molière's *Ecole des Femmes*) in 1961. The production was by another leading Scottish actor, Tom Fleming. In 1964, Walter Carr was produced by Victor Carin in another translation of Molière, *The Hypochondriack*, and gave a performance which Robert Kemp described as brilliant. He has played grimly realistic Glasgow parts on the legitimate stage, notably in Roddie MacMillan's *All In Good Faith*, where he played the lead originally created by the author.

110

Walter Carr has a slight physical resemblance to Tommy Lorne and Duncan Macrae, yet is quite different from both of them, but it is evident that he can play variety-style comedy as giftedly as the straight stuff.

A young artist who used to switch from tap dancing and choreography to fitting in with comedy parts in the McLean sketches was Desmond Carroll—real name, Arthur Fellows, of a well-known Glasgow musical family. Later he tried comedy with another team, and eventually settled into production. He did a great burlesque of ballet with Betty Bright, and his "Highland" tap dance was magnificent.

Glen Daly was another of the McLean feeds who was an act in himself, both as a comic and as a straight singer. A fair-haired, chubby-faced Glasgow Irishman, Glen is as enthusiastic for Irish as for Scottish songs. He can give a complete act of the songs of Robert Burns and also have the ancient Hibernians weeping with his airs from across the Irish Sea. Dan Campbell of the Palladium used to have a great admiration for Glen's voice and singing style, and Dan knew something about that side of show business. Eventually Glen went off to stand on his own feet, and he is still going strong as vocalist and stand-up comedian, and as the leader in shows.

The feed *par excellence* is Colin Murray, supporting his wife Grace Clark in their always entertaining act of songs at the piano. Colin is the well-dressed stooge, admirably adapted to Grace's style of comedy, much of which one suspects he helps to think up. Grace derives a great deal of her laughter-making from her asides about Colin—"the wee sowl," as she calls him. Clark and Murray is a grand survivor of the days when double acts were the mainstay of our variety programmes—Hope and Lang, Pagan and Ross, Power and Bendon and so on, all acts with some quality of their own, ringing the changes on repartee and the contrast of personalities.

Martin and Holbein was one such act in the thirties. They were Pete and Charlie Halfpenny, two brothers who had worked in the shipyards (source of so many of our Clydeside comedians). Pete was the straight man and Charlie Holbein was the sad-faced comic, whose expression was so naturally amusing that he did not need make-up but was as funny to look at as a painted clown. Charlie died and Pete carried on as a comic and lead in revue. They were associated with a singing and dancing act, the Thomson Sisters, in the jazz age and the hey-day of Scottish seaside entertainers.

Some of the straight actors who have found opportunities on the variety and panto stage have been useful feeds, men such as Clement

111

Ashby and Glen Michael who are capable of a wide range of stock character parts in comic sketches.

Now Glen Michael has become an accomplished and popular presenter of programmes on TV and radio, and has a fund of topical and other comical allusions to liven up the rests between musical items.

The great Tommy Lorne had a number of feeds, but the two I remember most are Harry Niblock, the "wee man," and W. S. Percy. They could not have been more different, except that both were below Tommy's height and helped to throw his gangling, skinny tallness into relief. Harry was a typical undersized Glaswegian, whom Tommy could call "ye wee nyaff" (this is a Scottish form of the English word *knave*, originally meant a servant or scullion, but is used in Scotland, especially in Glasgow, to describe a small person who tends to be bumptious and over-bearing).

Niblock played that part of the bossy little type, and sometimes he was a gangster or a cowboy with two six-shooters telling Tommy: "I'll fill ye fulla lead." A Dangerous Dan McGrew with a Glasgow accent was always good for a laugh, especially with big Tommy in the desperate confrontation.

W. S. Percy, on the other hand, was a cultured Englishman, with a long and distinguished record in musical comedy and legitimate acting. His refinement set off Tommy's Glasgowness much as Bret Harte's affected Kelvinside set off the gallus Gallowgate of Dora Lindsay.

Bret Harte was another of the great stooges, really a leading comedian in discreet disguise. He could be the comic of the show, but his best role was that of the straight man. He was a comedian who could act entirely without script. He had stored in his head a lot of traditional material, and could carry any comedian on the stage. He was the main support of Tommy Lorne when that genius started on the Princess stage in the Gorbals, and George West, who had such a long run in Princess shows when Tommy made the big time, must have learned a great deal from Bret Harte.

George West also passed on a lot of the tradition to other comics. He was stocked up with all the situations and used to tell me: "Anything you want to know about pantomime, come and ask me! I think I know most of the gags." George West at one time wrote panto scripts for other shows on the road.

Frank Droy, husband and partner of Doris, was another of the perfect feeds, and also a script-writer. The Queen's pantos were at one time largely of his devising. He was in the Bret Harte tradition, saturated

112

with comedy material, and he also knew what made working-class Scots, and especially Glaswegians, rock with laughter. He also knew his comics, and particularly his "Suicide Sal."

The pair of them, as they proved when they crossed the Border and performed in the North of England, were not so purely local after all; but when they were in Glasgow, they were the great interpreters of the spirit of the city.

Jack Anthony was another comic who derived strength from his feeds, particularly Bond Rowell, really a straight actor who was good at Bad Barons, Alderman Fitzwarrens, and Dames, and Bertha Ricardo, a blonde soubrette who was the wife of a prominent Glasgow hotelier and later managed Jack Anthony's hotel at Dunbar.

Dave Willis had a great feed in Cliff Harley, again an accomplished artist who could produce several entertaining acts of his own. Jack Holden, who could make £13 a week on his own in the cinemas in the twenties, when that "wasn't hay," was a staunch foil to Harry Gordon. He was particularly brilliant in front-cloth double acts with the wee Aberdonian. Again there was some physical contrast, for Holden in the kilt looked like a Highland athlete and made Harry look diminutive.

Tommy Hope was a Tommy Morgan support, and also a star on his own in *Seaside Follies* which Morgan presented in the thirties. Tommy Yorke also fed Morgan, and likewise starred as leading comic on occasion.

One of the best supporting comics from the West of Scotland is John Mulvaney, who was in many Jimmy Logan shows and latterly has been associated with Johnny Beattie. Mulvaney has an amusing line of rapid-fire, "sweetiewife" patter, delivered with the breathlessness of a garrulous small boy. In the shows in which "silly Jimmy Logan" was featured in classroom slapstick, Johnny Mulvaney was an essential character support.

Jack Raymond was another Tommy Morgan support, who was highly rated as an artist on his own in the circuits in the twenties.

"A comedian's labourer" was how one of these feeds described himself. The comedian is the front man for all sorts of people, including producers and script writers, but if he is a true comedian he is unlikely to find any of them indispensible. On the whole, they are more easily replaced than he is, as in the long run it is his genius in delivery that makes the joke, so far as the audience is concerned.

Most comics also have well stocked minds, as illustrated in such

113

programmes as *Jokers Wild* and *Does the Team Think?* Gags come naturally to them. Nevertheless they are glad of the services of script-writers. Some scriptwriters, like the feeds, decide to be front men them-selves, but even a comedian with a talent for scriptwriting will be glad to enlist other scriptwriters to freshen up his material.

Harry Gordon is a case in point. Harry wrote many of his own scripts and songs, yet he was always on the look-out for other scriptwriters who suited his style of humour. And, as a scriptwriter himself, Gordon was always scrupulous to pay other writers for their trouble. He was a squareshooter, something that cannot be said of all artists. Some of them, even when they hit the big time, seem still to be haunted by the spectre of the poverty they left behind on the way up, for they grudge paying for their material. People who write scripts for comedians soon find out the good payers and the artists to avoid.

It was Harry Gordon who started Joan Benyon on her scriptwriting career in the forties. Her late husband, Tom, a Warwickshire man who went out to British Columbia in his teens to work on a cattle farm, acted with George Arliss in *Disraeli* on tour and took part in such silent films as *The Exploits of Elaine* (with Pearl White) and *A Fool There Was* (with the vamp, Theda Bara), gravitated to Edinburgh King's as wartime manager when invalided out of the Royal Artillery. He and Joan had married in India. In Edinburgh, Joan wrote a lyric which Tom showed to Harry Gordon, then the star of the resident summer show. Harry said, "I'll take it," and promptly paid for it. The comedian encouraged her to go on with that type of work, and, after the war, scriptwriting and a theatrical agency gave them a living.

Another of the strict paying customers on Mrs Benyon's list is Jimmy Logan. I have myself worked with Jimmy, who generally has an idea of what he is after, and, in a script conference, acts out the character he intends to portray. Ian Gourlay, the Glasgow musician and orchestral arranger, has written a few numbers for Jimmy, as for other artists, along with Cliff Hanley and other lyrists. Ian's best comedians' song, for a double act, is *Andy McKay and Sandy McKay*.

It is difficult for comedians to keep material as their own property, or at least it was difficult in the days of the circuits, when one comic was sometimes able to listen to another's act from the wings, and memorise the best gags, which he might be able to use in some other theatre if their paths diverged. Once, not long before Edinburgh Empire went over to bingo, I heard Jack Radcliffe in a show there. He said: "The warders at Peterhead are threatening to strike because Ramensky is getting more holidays than they are." I thought this was a good joke to tell at Saughton Prison, where I was lecturing to prisoners soon after.

Ramensky, alias John Ramsay, was a notorious safe-blower, who had a talent also for escaping from Peterhead, Barlinnie, and any other jail he happened to be doing time in. He was always in the headlines with some new escapade.

I told the story at Saughton, and the prison officers laughed as much as the prisoners. Shortly afterwards I was taking Jimmy Logan, who had kindly agreed to talk to the prisoners, to Saughton, the series having been arranged by Sandy Trotter, ex-editor and chairman of the *Scottish Daily Express*.

On the way, Jimmy asked me if I thought he could crack a joke which he proceeded to tell me. It was the one about Ramensky. I said: "There would be no objection to that joke, except that I've already cracked it at Saughton."

"Where the dickens did *you* get it?" he asked.

I replied: "I heard Jack Radcliffe crack it at the Empire here."

"The devil you did!" exclaimed Jimmy: "It's my joke."

However, we went on to the jail, where Jimmy experienced the talent for jokes of some of the prisoners. He got a team of them to lift a piano on to the platform and sat down to play and sing to them. When he asked: "Any requests?" one of them immediately shouted out: "Show me the way to go home!" and another prisoner followed up with: "Don't fence me in!"

Edinburgh actually has a monument to a scriptwriter whose song has been on everybody's lips since the middle of the war. It is not a big monument but it is quite prominently placed at the top of the Mound and the foot of Lady Stair's Close, opposite the statue of the Black Watch soldier which overlooks Princes Street. It is one of the seats which Edinburgh Corporation welcomes from public-spirited citizens who choose this way of commemorating people they have admired. The plate on it gives the name of Johnnie J. Kerr, the shy man who wrote Dave Willis's ARP song, *In My Wee Gas Mask*. There is almost a case for raising a monument to the Unknown Scriptwriter, though nowadays plenty of writers are given their credits on the air and in *Radio Times* and *TV Times*.

It is relatively easy to keep a hold on the performing rights of songs, thanks to the Performing Rights Society, and also sketches; but jokes go into circulation rapidly and are regarded as everybody's property, even when a gag writer has worked hard on them.

I have been amused to follow the careers of some of my own jokes. In the middle of the war I was on a bus from Rutherglen to Bridgeton Olympia Cinema, where I had to give a Sunday night Ministry of Information lecture. I was wondering what to say, to put my audience in a good mood, and I thought of telling them a funny story.

It was the days when whisky was being rationed, and an American soldier, out for a drink, became annoyed because, in every pub he walked into, the barman stuck up a notice: "Whisky Off." The American said: "Aw, to hell with Britain!" and a customer standing at his elbow emmediately punched him on the chin so that he hit the sawdust.

Picking himself up and dusting himself down, the American asked: "What the hell did you do that for?"

"Well," said the Scotsman, "what was it you said just now?"

"Hell!" expostulated the Yank: "I just said 'To hell with Britain!'"

"Oh, I'm sorry," said the Scot: "I thought you said: 'To hell with Brigton!'" (That is what the people of Bridgeton call their district.)

My story got a good laugh and won me a very receptive audience in that reputedly tough locality. Being a Scot, I did not like to waste a good joke, so I put it into the gossip column I was then writing for the *Glasgow Evening News*, called *Talk of the Town*.

A few nights later I was at a meeting in a Services canteen where James Bridie (Dr Mavor), the famous playwright, was called upon to speak. I was flattered to hear him tell my story, and very well he told it.

The following week I lifted the *Glasgow Evening News* and there was my story in yet another column of the paper, *Clydeside Echoes*. I spoke to the colleague who was writing that column, and asked him where he had got the story. He had been told it at a golf club. He was quite incredulous when I told him that I had made up the story, and that I had already put it into the same paper. (We journalists are not devout readers of one another's columns.)

Another story I saw go the rounds was one I made up to tell at a dinner attended by a number of Highlanders. It was of the Elgin man who heard his son was going on a mission to the Indonesians, and he frowned and said: "I am very sorry you are going among people like that."

"Why, father?" asked the son: "What do you know against the Indonesians?"

"Oh," said the father, "I thought you said 'Invernesians'."

Needless to say, this story was particularly appreciated in Inverness, which proves that the Scottish ability to take a joke is fairly widespread.

Most gags are adaptations of traditional ones. I do not profess to be a wit like Oscar Wilde or Sir Noel Coward, but I have occasionally been inspired to make an apt comment off the top of my head. I was at a Post Office Telephones lunch commemorating the centenary of Alexander Graham Bell, the inventor of the telephone. It was held in the Roxburgh Hotel, opposite Bell's birghplace in Charlotte Street, Edinburgh.

The chef had made telephones with meringues for the ear and mouth pieces, and when a telephones man drew my attention to them I could not resist saying: "That's where I get meringue numbers."

It came to me in a flash; but it was not entirely original. In my mind was the tale of the piper who was asked: "Will you have a whisky or a meringue?" and replied: "Ye're richt." (A meringue—Am I wrang?)

14

The Brain Drain

ALTHOUGH so many Scotch comics have been able to survive, and some of them to make a fair living, without having to go out of Scotland very often, most of them have had occasional tours abroad and round England and other parts of these islands. And more Scots than we realise have scored as comics outside of Scotland and not as Scotch comedians at all. Even Lauder, when he first appeared in England at the Argyle in Birkenhead, was an "Irish comedian," singing a song in which he had collaborated, *Call Again Callaghan*. When he got to London he decided to shake off the Irish label and revert to his true nationality. Conversely, Talbot O'Farrell, who became accepted as an Irish comedian and singer (he was a Lancashire man), tried his hand before that as a Scotch comedian under the name Bill MacIver.

After them, the next Scot to turn up as a success on the London music halls was seldom regarded as a Scotsman at all, and he allowed it to be assumed that he was an Irishman. He was Charles Coburn, who became famous for his song, *The Man That Broke the Bank at Monte Carlo*.

His real name was Colin Whitton McCallum, son of Colin McCallum of Bunchrew, Inverness, a shipbroker and freeman of the city of London.

He began in commerce in London's city in 1866, when he was only 14, and became a professional music-hall artist when he was 20. He performed in seaside shows and even busked between engagements, and he made the London Pavilion in 1880. Another of his famous songs was *Two Lovely Black Eyes*, but his Monte Carlo song even took him on to the screen. In addition to being the first of the great song pluggers, Charles Coburn was a great long-distance walker, including walks to Land's End and John o' Groats. One of his sons was Tory M.P. for Argyllshire, Sir Duncan MacCallum. Charles Coburn, who died in November 1945, is generally thought to have done only dude numbers, but in fact he was a great Cockney singer as well.

Another comedian who was regarded even in Scotland as an English turn, Harry Tate, was a Scot. His real name was Ronald Macdonald Hutchinson. He began his music-hall career as a mimic, then developed his "silly ass," dude part, with his long, propeller moustache, and sporty clothes, and his motoring, golfing, and fishing sketches which took him on tour for many years. Acts lasted artists longer in those days before TV. He appeared also in revue and panto. His yodelling "Good-bye-ee!" became everybody's catchword. Tate died in 1940, aged 66, after making Britain laugh from the early years of the century.

In the Julie Andrews film of the life of Gertrude Lawrence, there was a reference to Jack Buchanan in America as an "Englishman." Well, of course, Jack, besides having a Scottish clan name, was born in Helensburgh, just on the Highland line, and old Glasgow theatregoers remembered him as a struggling dancer and singer at Pickard's Panopticon in the Trongate, Glasgow, where a long stick with a hook on it was used to haul artists off the stage when they got the bird, which was quite often. But Jack soon made the big time in London, and by the middle of the Great War he was famous as Dudley Mitten in *Tonight's the Night*, and thereafter was in great demand in London revue and musical comedy, eventually breaking into films.

Charlot's Revue took him to New York in 1926 and he was an accepted star in the States from then on. Like Stanley Baxter and Tom Fleming, he played Elwood P. Dowd in *Harvey*, but Buchanan played it in the 48th Street Theatre in New York.

At least one well-known screen comic, Andy Clyde, was a Scot, one of the family of a famous actor of Rob Roy and other Scott parts, John Clyde. Stan Laurel was an Englishman, but he had part of his upbringing in Rutherglen, Lanarkshire, when his father—the real name was Jefferson —was managing the old Metropole, formerly the Scotia, in Stockwell

119

Street, Glasgow. Old Ruglonians remembered Stan as a boy performing on his own fit-up stage in Stonelaw Drive for the entertainment of the locals. He went to the States with the Fred Karno *Mumming Birds* (called there *A Night in an English Music-Hall*) and, when Mack Sennett bagged Charles Chaplin for films in Holywood, Hal Roach engaged Stan.

That great actor and comedian, and now chronicler of variety and its personnel, Georgie Wood, had part of his schooling in Scotland and he has an affection for some of Scotland's old comics, on whom he is an authority. Recently in his highly readable regular column in *The Stage*, Georgie referred to Alex Munro as "this little Scottish dynamo of comedy." Alex Munro, like Peter Sinclare, who supported the late Jimmy Clitheroe in his radio series, keeps up the Scotch comic tradition south of the Border.

"He is deservedly popular locally," added Georgie, referring to Alex's "funny and clean" act in Lancashire and Wales, "and they stress he proves that it is possible to be a humorous *family* funmaker." Alex's music-hall season at Llandudno Pier runs from the beginning of May right into October.

Now Ronnie Corbett, an Edinburgh man, stars on TV and is not typed as a Scotch comic. In the Dick Hurran panto, *Cinderella* (1972-3), at Bristol Hippodrome (Sonny Zahl Kavanagh Entertainments announced) half the population of the city paid £135,141 to see this little Scot play Buttons. His appearances on the BBC screen with Ronnie Barker, *The Two Ronnies* and in his own show *Now Look Here*, with Rosemary Leach, have been highly rated. Ronnie's wife Anne, an actress and singer, became his feed in his act in a London night club. They worked together for seven years before marrying and starting a family.

Ronnie was a scholar of Edinburgh Royal High School, and his townie, Roy Kinnear, another who does not appear as a Scotch comic, went to George Heriot's School. Roy, a naturally funny "roly-poly" character, has proved, in a revival of almost-silent films, that he has a genius for mime. He would have been a natural for the movies before talking and singing began to spoil them.

15

The Scotch Joke

WHAT makes people laugh, and why? Philosophers, psychologists, anthropologists, evolutionists—they all have a go at explaining. Bergson, Erasmus, Freud, Charles Darwin—many are their theories of laughter, and while each of them seems to hit on something near the truth, humour is still a great mystery, and the place of the comedian in society is still a matter for wide speculation.

William Willeford, in *The Fool and His Sceptre*: *A Study in Clowns and Jesters and Their Audience* (London: Edward Arnold, 1969), deals at length with the cult and magic importance of the clown in some parts of the world. Even in dour, Calvinistic Scotland, the comedian is a kind of warlock who can hold audiences spellbound and trick them into laughter.

He performs a kind of Indian rope trick in which he disappears up a hole in his own head. He is a shaman and a medicine man. If he is good at his mysterious trade, you will hear the audience say: "He's a tonic."

All these philosophical, anthropological, and psychiatric references to clowns and comics make it evident that there are universal themes of humour, and it would be rather foolish of us Scots to claim that our own comedy is unique. But there are certain peculiarities, there are particular Scotch jokes, and our approach to the universal themes is as national as

121

our tartan, our whisky, and our porridge. So, if I discuss Scotch humour, I hope it will not be thought that I am ignorant of the fact that many of our jokes have their counterparts in other cultures, even in England— a country of such close proximity, though marked difference, with which we naturally trade a great deal in ideas, as well as in solid and liquid commodities.

Let me dispose first of all of the obvious Scotch joke—the one about meanness. This joke is not so popular among Scottish audiences as might be supposed, but we keep it up to entertain the foreigner, especially the Englishman. It belongs partly to one of the universal types of joke noted by the anthropologists—the burlesquing of foreigners. It is a handy racial joke for the English against the Scots. The Scotch comedian, especially to an English or other Anglo-Saxon audience, will use it just as a Jewish comic might use an anti-Jewish joke to a Gentile audience, or a Negro might use a joke about his colour to a white audience, because he knows he will get a quick laugh.

The Jew does not do it to encourage anti-Semitism. He probably thinks that it will have the opposite effect of disarming the racialist.

Similarly the Negro comic who pipes up: "Was my face red?" knows that he floors the "ofay" who considers his colour inferior. Sammy Davis Junior turns it into an anti-white joke by pretending that the audience thinks he is Harry Belafonte, and saying in an aside, in a fruity upper-class English voice: "You can't tell them apart, actually."

So also the Scot, telling an anti-Scottish joke, is simultaneously satirising the Englishman's ignorant assumption that all Scots are alike— and all as mean as a starling with a leatherjacket.

But there must be another reason than the professional Scotch comic's offering of himself up as a foreigner to be burlesqued. Certainly Sir Harry Lauder, by telling mean jokes about himself or allowing them to be circulated, and wearing the kilt comically and carrying a funny walking-stick, deliberately set himself up as a foreigner for the Anglo-Saxon to laugh at. The kilt has always been something for Anglo-Saxons to laugh at, God bless them! The mean joke has a shorter and more intriguing history.

It really came into circulation, as affecting the Scots, in Victorian times, though the ridicule and satirising of Scots has been an English game for many generations. Some English writers, notably Charles Churchill and Dr Samuel Johnson, made themselves famous for anti-Scottish witticisms. But neither Churchill nor Johnson uses the mean joke. Some writers ridiculed the Scot for coming south and battening on the English, for being poor and having the itch (scabies was endemic in the Highlands in the eighteenth century, and even Prince Charlie joked, when wearing Highland dress: "All I need now is the itch, and I'll be a complete Highlander"). But a joke about the Scotsman's meanness had not arrived.

It was *Punch*, and particularly the cartoonist Charles Keene, that popularised the joke about the Scot's meanness. And the strange thing is that Keene got many of his jokes from a kind Scotsman—in Aberdeen of all places—who admired his drawings and postcarded him with ideas. What he was sending him, in fact, was a series of traditional North Country and Highland jokes about mean men.

In Scotland the mean man has always been a figure of ridicule, precisely because hospitality and generosity are strong Scottish traditions. "Highland hospitality" is well-known. It is rooted in the addiction of the Celt to *potlach*, a rivalry in generosity, noted by Henri Hubert in *The Rise of the Celts* and *The Greatness and Decline of the Celts*.

In old Gaelic poetry (preserved in *The Book of the Dean of Lismore*), you will find the generous chiefs praised and the ungenerous ones savagely ridiculed, and there is one long, humorous poem about a scrounger who collected everything he could lay his hands on. Scotland was perhaps a poor country, and thrift a natural virtue, but the selfish man and the moocher were alike figures of fun.

This is the secret of the Aberdeen Joke Factory. Aberdeen is the home of hospitality and warm-heartedness, and if you want to hear a good joke about a mean person you will hear it in Aberdeen. Harry Gordon was a most generous man, but he enjoyed pretending to be a close-fisted Aberdonian.

Punch, being a comic paper, and one with a big appeal to the English gentry, inevitably burlesqued the Scots with whom its readers came in contact on hunting, shooting, and fishing holidays. Hence the old *Punch* cartoons of red-nosed, tartan-clad, whiskered gillie types, often depicted in driving rain on heather and whin-clad slopes. Jokes about drink, ministers, and parsimoniousness helped to sustain the flow of gillie cartoons—and most of these jokes are of Scottish origin: Scotland's gift to the English! Lauder cashed in on their popularity in the South.

So long as these jokes are regarded as referring to mean individuals, and not assumed to be typical of our people, they are more than acceptable to us. Lowlanders may dodge the national reference by localising the stories in Aberdeen, which is rather a dirty trick; but perhaps the North-Eastern city has only itself to blame for circulating them.

Some of these stories are clever, and have a depth of meaning. The best is probably that of the father whose boy fell into Aberdeen Harbour, and was rescued by a stranger. The hero was a shy man who tried to disappear through the cheering crowd, but was pointed out to the boy's father. The father pursued him and took a tight grip of his wet lapel, asking: "Are you the man that saved my laddie out of the harbour?"

Shyly the hero admitted that he was, whereat the father demanded:

"Weill, far's (where's) his bonnet?"

My own favourite is of the Aberdonian who was passing Register House in Princes Street, Edinburgh, when a young man approached him and asked for a match. The Northerner produced a box of matches from his pocket and handed it over.

"That's perfect," said the stranger, surprisingly: "Do you know you're in luck? I am on a sales-promotion campaign, and my job is to give a pound to the first man who shows me a box of these particular matches. You are now the proud possessor of a crisp new one-pound note!"

Without more ado, he placed the pound in the hand of the astonished Aberdonian, turned on his heel, and walked away.

The man from the Granite City looked at the money for a moment in bewilderment, then suddenly cried: "Hi, come back! I knew there was a catch in it! Ye're awa' wi' my matches."

Anti-clerical humour goes back in Scotland to pre-Reformation times, as witness *The Thrie Estaites* and *The Friars of Berwick*. Now the butt is usually the ordinary Presbyterian minister, who is often portrayed in comic sketches. Along with him go the elders and the beadle.

A minister and an elder went calling on parishioners. Mrs Macpherson made them a cup of tea and handed out her best home-made scones. They tucked into them with relish. The elder, showing off in front of the minister, started to catechise Mrs Macpherson.

"What do you think," he asked, "of the story of the miracle of the loaves and fishes?"

"I dinna ken," said she, "but I'll tell ye this—if you and the minister had been there, there wadna have been a' thae baskets o' crumbs."

A minister met one of his elders and was shocked to find him intoxicated. He rebuked him with "I thought you were a teetollar." The elder replied: "So I am, but I'm no' a bigoted one."

The minister said he should be an example to the flock, and the elder said: "Minister, it's doing my duty by the kirk that has landed me in this condition. I was handing round the communion cards, and you know how hospitable our parishioners are—every house I went in they gave me a dram."

"Do you mean to tell me," harangued the minister, "that we have no teetotallers on our communion roll?"

"Oh ay," smiled the elder, "there's teetotallers a' right, but I just send their cards through the post."

The minister thought it best to see the elder home. As they entered the house, the elder's wife was heard crying down the stair: "Drunk again, John?" and the elder replied: "Ay, and ye'll never guess who I've been with."

Probably related to this obsession with religion and the life beyond is Lex McLean's favourite routine: "Why worry? There are only two things to worry about—whether you're well or you're ill. If you're well you've nothing at all to worry about, and if you're ill you've only two things to worry about—whether you're gonny live or die. If you're gonny live you've nothing whatever to worry about and if you're gonny die you've only two things to worry about—whether you're going up there or down there. If you're going up there you've nothing whatever to worry about, and if you're going down there, you'll be that busy shaking hands with all your friends, you'll have nae time to worry."

Death is a favourite subject of comedy in Scotland. Rikki Fulton wrote and performed in a sketch at Edinburgh Gateway, in his apprentice days, in which he was visiting a friend in hospital, played by the straight actor, John Young. Rikki fired off a succession of lugubrious jokes of the type of "This'll be an awkward kind of place to get a coffin out of."

When he left his friend with a pile of magazines, he said: "Ye better no' get started on the serials."

This sketch—one death crack after another—had the Gateway audience helpless.

Once I was asked on radio, in front of an English studio audience, to give a typical Scottish story, and I told the one about the minister walking along the street and seeing a solemn procession of small boys marching along the kerbside. He was curious to know what they were playing at, and he asked the boy in front: "What game is this, sonny?"

"It's a funeral," answered the boy without smiling.

"Oh," said the minister, "that's sad. Who's dead?"

"Dinna ask *me*," said the boy: "I'm the horse."

This brought instant laughter of the deep type, and I was surprised at the number of people on both sides of the Border who later told me they had heard me tell the story. It is long since funeral horses were a familiar sight in the streets, even in Scotland, but the joke still seems to click. This was a favourite story of the late Jack Radcliffe's.

Jack—and Jim Jessiman before him—played the music-hall sketch in which as a drunkard he was dressed in a white gown by his wife, and his face painted to look like a skull, to cure him of drinking. When he came out of his stupor, everyone pretended he was dead, and no one answered his questions. When they were gone he looked at himself in the mirror and received a terrible shock.

His small boy, who had not been let into the deception, came in and spoke to his father. I can still hear Jim Jessiman telling the little boy sadly—and most ridiculously—"You've no Daddy now."

I seem to remember Dave Willis performing the same sketch, which always appealed to the sepulchral humour of the Scots audiences. It is closely linked to the origins of Halloween and Hogmanay guising, the Festival of the Dead, in which the departed were supposed to come back from beyond. *Tam o' Shanter* is full of such jokes about death and the Devil, suggesting the mystical roots of our clowning.

As for humour based on sex and obscenity, another universal classification noted by Julian H. Steward in *The Ceremonial Buffoon of the American Indian*, Scotch comedians are reputed to be clean. It would be a ludicrous pretence to try to claim that Scottish humour is completely free from smut. Robert Burns may have cleaned up some rather rough songs for use in the polite salon, and for ladies to sing, but the same man collected some of the crude originals, and other obscenities perpetuated in *The Merry Muses of Caledonia*, and there is a good deal of sexual humour in older Scottish literature.

Sir Harry Lauder did not use crude sex jokes or "blue" material in his act, but Will Fyffe's *Ninety-Four Today* has discreet jests about age and sex, and in his ploughman act there was a silhouette of his girl friend undressing in a lighted room behind a blind.

It was the sort of unembarrassing sex reference to which we were accustomed on the music-hall stage before this permissive age, when there were still family shows in which any sexual allusions went completely over the heads of the younger members of the audience. Yet in 1932 Fyffe walked out of Earl Carroll's *Vanities* on Broadway because it had too much sex.

Without being technically obscene, Scottish comedy plays a lot around the differences between the sexes, and the war between the sexes. The typical music-hall sketch is a battle of wits between the man of the house

126

and the wife who wants to be the head of the house; or it is the classical dilemma of a married man trying to hide an affaire from his wife. Adultery may just have been discovered by the pornographers, but it was a stage theme from Shakespeare's time to the present day, allusive rather than in the overt manner of the X film.

However, in funny story and in stage situation-comedy, the sex theme takes more often the shape of the battle for mastery between man and woman. It is also a favourite theme of the Scots newspaper cartoonist, as is the conflict between neighbour wives. There is the husband who admits that his wife controls the children, the cat, and the canary, but he can say what he likes to the goldfish. And the one who has three controls on his TV—his wife, his daughter, and his mother-in-law. But the Scot also likes to pretend that he is a dominating husband. Sometimes, too, the sex joke of the cleaner sort is crossed with the meanness jest.

There is the tale of the North countryman who took sweets to his girl friend every Saturday. After marriage, there were no more sweets. Said Maggie: "Ye never bring me hame yon candy ye used to bring when we were just gaun thegither."

"Na," said the canny lad, "a man does-na bait the hook efter he's caught the fish."

The Scots husband's alleged fondness for a dram too many is represented as the most common cause of dispute. Perhaps the dram is to give him courage, as Will Fyffe sang in *I Belong to Glasgow*, to "speak back to the wife."

"My wife kisses me every time I come home," says the comic.

"Is that affection?"

"No, investigation."

There was a knock at the door and Mrs Macgregor answered it.

"Could you give anything to the Inebriates' Home?" asked the stranger.

"Come back at eleven," she replied, "and I'll gie ye Jock."

The husband returning home three sheets in the wind and defying his wife, and perhaps even his mother-in-law, has formed the theme for many sketches. Most Scotch comics have featured a drunk act in their repertoire.

One wife told her husband: "Ye've just drunk three glasses o' whisky. I couldna drink that quantity o' water."

"Na," said he, "neither could I."

Marriage in the Scottish joke can be mixed, as if in a cocktail, with financial gain and the national obsession with death:

127

One old farmer had been married once or twice and each time his wife had brought him some money. A friend remarked: "Ye'll be makin' something out o' this," but he replied: "I dinna ken aboot that. By the time ye tak them up and pit them doon there's nae that muckle left."

A minister was surprised at a widowed parishioner marrying for a third time. The old stager said: "But, minister, I just thocht it would be nice to have a young wife to close my eyes when I die."

"My man," replied the minister, "I've had two, and they've both opened mine."

Two young Glasgow lads were sitting in a bus when a pretty girl came in and sat down near them. She gave one of the young men a friendly look.

"That's Jeanie McGraw," he said. "I think I'll go and speak to her. She's a wee smasher."

"Haud on!" said his pal. "Dinna be in such a hurry. Wait till she's paid her fare!"

There are naturally many Scottish golfing stories, as Scotland is a country which claims the origin of golf. There is the one of the man about to take a tricky putt on a green near the main road. A funeral came by, and he stopped to stand with head uncovered until it passed. His opponent remarked: "I did not think you were so respectful as all that."

He replied: "Man, it was the least I could dae. She's been a good wife to me."

Reverting to Will Fyffe's version of the sex theme, the old man's defiance of the passing years, there is a story which may be universal but which appeals mightily to Scots:

One septuagenarian consulted his doctor about his plan to marry a very young woman. The doctor said: "There's nothing to stop you, but if I were you I'd keep a lodger."

Some time later he met the old man and asked how his marriage was going along. "Fine," said the old man: "My wife's expecting."

The doctor smiled and asked: "Did ye take a lodger?"

"Ay," replied the veteran: "*She's* expecting, tae."

A hardened old reprobate turned up in the Glasgow court.

Said the magistrate: "I see you've been fighting with your wife. Liquor again?"

"Na," he pleaded: "This time *she* licked *me*."

Another man, in a higher court, was asked by the judge: "Do you know the penalty for bigamy?"

"Ay," said the defender, "two mothers in law."

128

Scots humour tends to be hard on the womenfolk.

The doctor jokes come into another of Steward's universal themes of humour, that based on sickness, sorrow, and misfortune. Perhaps the death theme which crops up in so many Scots jokes belongs to this grouping. But misfortune is a natural subject in a country where the struggle for a livelihood has often been severe.

Even the prosperous Scot can have a setback—like MacNab, who was so tired of hearing the mean Scotch joke in a Broadway saloon that he stood drinks to everybody in the bar. He took a heart attack soon after when he learned that they had all imagined he was an Irishman.

I have mentioned the tendency to laugh at the folk whose misfortune it is to be smaller than the average. Wee Shewie (Hugh) is the mythical small character of Scotland, and he is usually in the predicament of being at the same time "Big Aggie's man." On the other hand, there is the equally ridiculous situation of the big man who is pushed about by the wee woman.

Once, in Glasgow, I saw this situation, in real life, cause laughter on the top of an electric tram going along London Road from Glasgow Cross to Bridgeton Cross. The tram pulled up to avoid an accident, because there was a street fracas in progress rather near the carriageway. It was a wee shawlie wife lamming into a huge muscular man of the Irish labourer type, outside a pub which had just turned its customers out on to the pavement.

A typical Glasgow working man a couple of seats in front of me laughed aloud and exclaimed: "'Sa help ma Goad! There's only wan thing a wumman's feart for, and that's a moose!"

He did not mean the great American elk, but the little, universal, house mouse.

In this category of humour, laughing at another's discomfiture, there is all the sadistic slating of athletes, which seems to be part of the enjoyment of a contest for many spectators. In boxing, all-in wrestling, and particularly Association football, the favourite sport of the working masses, the character on the seats or the terracing who keeps up a running commentary on the match seems to be an indispensable adjunct of the sport. It suggests that the athlete is in much the position of the comic butt, he who gets slapped—he is there for the satisfaction of some cruel streak in the nature of the general public.

Our Scotch comics often portray the Soccer terracing commentator, in a routine describing the game as it proceeds, and making devastating comments on players and referee.

I was at a boxing show in Parkhead, Glasgow, before the last war, where the referee gave an unpopular decision and was booed as he left the ring. The same referee was announced for the next fight, and this had not proceeded very far when he narrowly avoided being run down by a retreating boxer. The inevitable voice from the crowd cried out: "Watch the blind man!" It released terrific laughter from the tensed-up crowd.

A Soccer team, even a favourite local one, which is having a bad streak, is always a handy theme for the comic in his topical stand-up routine. Lex McLean is a Rangers supporter, but his loyalty to the club is not allowed to interfere with his savagely amusing cracks about it, and about individual players, when he gets up in front of the curtain. And I am sure that he obtains his greatest response from Rangers followers in the audience.

Chronic misfortunes or illnesses, it might be thought, ought not to be the object of laughter, yet the main stock in trade of the clown is the knowledge that people will laugh at sheer stupidity and mental aberration. The clown acts the fool. When I was a boy I took a piece of charcoal from a camp fire and drew Charlie Chaplin on the flap of my tent. A Banffshire farmer stopped to look at it, and remarked drily: "Huh, Charlie Chaplin! He maks his money acting the goat."

He may have laughed at Chaplin in his day, but he evidently did not think the comedian should be paid for it.

The townsman laughs at the country yokel, and the country yokel laughs at the village natural. Everybody has to have somebody whom he can consider dafter than himself.

A wife gets her best laughs at her man's handlessness in domestic tasks. A husband laughs at what he thinks is the tinier brain of the woman.

Tommy Lorne, goofing about on the stage, was always apparently impressed by the brainlessness of some other character. His remark— "Here, the coos'll get ye!"—always caused a guffaw. He meant: "The cows will get you"—in other words, you don't know enough to run away from danger.

Just as a child gets satisfaction out of meeting a smaller and obviously less advanced baby, the clown in this situation expresses the hope of us all that we are cleverer than the next man.

In a less enlightened age, real-life fools were exploited for the merriment of the mob. Scotland had at least one famous one, in the North East— Feel (Fool) Jamie Fleeman, the Laird of Udny's fool. He was a simple lad to whom passers-by addressed questions in the hope of getting a funny reply. Often, in fact, he scored off the would-be superior questioner. When asked: "Are you the Laird of Udny's fool," he replied: "Ay, fa's feel are ee!" (Whose fool are *you*?)

A man who was cruelly exploited for public amusement in Scotland—and still is, long after his death in his native Edinburgh—was "Sir" William McGonagall, who discovered, when a weaver in Dundee, that he had a gift for rhyming, but was deaf to regular metrics. His *Poetic Gems* are still in circulation. McGonagall's chronic misfortune was that he had no sense of humour. As a barnstormer, and as a rhymer, he could be extremely disconcerting without having the slightest clue what they were all laughing at. He became the butt of students, apprentices, and other groups of merrymakers; but he made a little money out of it.

Many of the silly rhymes attributed to McGonagall, and quoted by comics with hilarious effect, are not really his. The production of fake McGonagalls became quite an industry, with such gems as:

"I saw a coo gaun doon the road:
It was a coo—a bull, b'Goad!"

McGonagall did not use broad dialect. Neither did he swear.

"Ships of war, painted with tar,
Sailing over the ocean potion."

That one was by an Edinburgh High Street poet, an habituee of the penny gaffs.

A favourite gag with Scottish beach pierrots, in the years before the Great War, was for the straight man, giving the comic advice about wooing his lady love, to suggest the first line of a Valentine:

"The rose's red, the violet's blue—"

and for the comic to finish it off with

"A bull has a horn and so has a coo."

It may be difficult to believe that this was considered funny, but it was.
Another fake McGonagall was:

"Dundee is a great city, famed for jute and jam,
And I'm the Great McGonagall, by Jiminy, I *am*!"

Still another:

"There were three men frae Mauchline cam:
Twa brocht eggs and ane brocht ham.
'Is it frae Mauchline that ye cam?'
'We am'."

But a Scotch comic could even get a laugh by just uttering the first line of "The cuddie rins aboot the braes," a well-known coarse rhyme about a donkey, which he never required to recite in full.

This is a Scottish equivalent of the old Cockney music-hall type of song in which innocuous words were substituted in the last line of each verse for the shocking rhyme which listeners anticipated. Such indecency as is used by Scottish entertainers publicly, is usually conveyed in this ever so slightly veiled form.

Several of our Scotch comedians have featured the village simpleton among their character acts. Lauder had a song, *The Saftest o' the Family*. Before him, J. C. Macdonald sang *Sandy Saft-a-Wee*. Will Fyffe's portrayal of the village lad used to move his audience to tears as well as to laughter. He evoked sympathy for the retarded boy, but he also had him scoring over the people who thought he was daft.

He carried a straw bag with a pheasant's tail protruding from it, and he showed that there was no bird at the end of the tail; but, he explained, this was for the benefit of the gamekeeper. That functionary imagined that the boy was simple enough to imagine that he had a pheasant in the bag, and when he saw the lad go by with the pheasant's tail protruding he just shook his head and laughed and passed on. By this means the youth was able to get away with a pheasant whenever he liked to poach one.

Lex McLean played this kind of fool much more realistically, but even he could arouse sentiment with his portrayal, while at the same time getting away with some near-the-knuckle humour.

Generally good taste draws the line at the ridiculing of some physical defects, but the comics make play with some peculiarities of speech, such as the watery lisp, the high-pitched masculine voice, the stutter, and confused manners of speaking, including the spoonerism and the malapropism.

In his *I Belong to Glasgow* routine, Fyffe used the spoonerism partly to suggest the effect of drink on the tongue and partly to illustrate the strain on the working-class speaker of attempting to attain a high standard of political oratory. He introduced also this example of confused thinking, explainable either by booze or by over-addiction to the complicated works of Karl Marx: "In the future we have been too slow but in the past we are going to show them what we're going to do." Not very funny in print, but the deliberate way in which Fyffe squeezed out his words, finishing with a frenzied gallop on the home stretch, made it comical.

There was the same affectation, followed by collapse, in his declaration of his right to speak as the "representatipive" of the British working man: "I have been deputed—and not only *deputed*, but *asked*!" Fyffe's voice rose and fell with effect.

The man with the piping voice evokes laughter by the suggestion that he has been castrated. Long before the present public obsession with homosexualism, the comic could win a laugh by calling his stooge a "Jessie," or addressing him as "Gladys."

Effeminacy was not necessarily associated with homosexualism. Even women in the audience, to whom the obscene suggestion would not occur, laughed at the man with the effeminate voice or manner.

Often, too, the comic would ape the gestures of a woman for a quick laugh. This has probably been part of miming through the ages. Neither this nor the practice of dressing up as the Dame and simulating, in caricature, the coy stratagems of womanhood, has anything to do with sexual aberration.

It is recognised that there is the type of boy who "should have been a lassie" and there is also the "sweetie-wife" type of man, such as the grocer's assistant who is so accustomed to talking to women in his store that he assimilates a lot of their speech and other mannerisms.

But when sex change was a prominent headline topic in the Press, it was natural that the comic should turn his partner's pretended effeminacy into a topical joke with an aside to the audience: "He's *changing*!"

Incidentally, Scottish dialect comedy is apt to founder on the fact that, even between Glasgow and Edinburgh, words are used with quite different meanings. In Glasgow a common stair is called a *close*, but in Edinburgh this word means an alley, and is almost confined to the old closes of the Royal Mile. In Glasgow a tiled stair is called a *wallie close*, and this phrase is scarcely understood in Edinburgh.

The Glasgow comic may say: "She's awfu' toffee-nosed because she stays in a wallie close." The word *wallie*—old Scots for an ornament—comes to mean anything of porcelain or resembling it, any ceramics such as a wall tile, and even false teeth, which are called *wallies*. A comic will tell his mumbling feed: "Ye better pit yer *wallies* back in." This again is pure Glescaranto, and Edinburgh audiences would need to be issued with phrasebooks.

George Elrick, the Aberdonian singer, band-leader, and impresario, once told me a true variant of the Scotch meanness joke. When he was in London in the forties, he was troubled with duodenal ulcer. He went to a Harley Street specialist, a famous titled consultant, whom he discovered to be also from the Granite City. The specialist took him to a hospital where the staff likewise were almost all Aberdeen folk. When it came to the question of a fee, they told him: "Don't bother paying: just send us a copy of every record you make."

At that time George already had made over 300 discs, and even at half-a-crown each that was a lot of money then. "A richt Aiberdeen trick!" was George Elrick's comment.

George was a collector of typical Scottish humour, especially of the drolleries of the North-East countryside. He used to quote the porter at Stonehaven station, who shouted to the passengers: "Here ye are for far ye're gaan, a' you 'at's in there for here, come oot, for this is it."

Another of his favourites was of the Buchan man in the railway carriage, who asked the taciturn stranger: "Are ye for Kintore?" to get the blunt reply: "No."

"Are ye for Kittybrewster, then?"

"No."

"Are ye for Aiberdeen?"

"No."

As he was getting out at his own station, the Buchan man turned back and asked the stranger indignantly: "Dae ye think I care a damn far ye're gaan?"

I heard a story once of a Buchan farmer travelling in a train and engaging the academic-looking stranger opposite in conversation. He made a remark about the land and the crops they were passing, and he gave the other a shrewd look, saying: "But ye'll nae ken muckle aboot the fermin'."

The stranger drew himself up and informed the rustic: "I'm a professor of agriculture."

The farmer laughed. "That means I'm richt," he said: "ye'll nae ken muckle aboot the fermin."

"I'll bet you a pound there isn't a question you could ask me about farming that I couldn't answer," said the professor, "if you'll give me a pound for any question I ask that will stump you."

"Na, na," answered the farmer, cannily. "Ye're an educated man: I'm juist an uneducated fermer. Tell ye what, mak it twa to ane. Ye gie me a pound if I stump ye, and I'll gie ye fifty pence if it's the ither road aboot."

The professor agreed and he asked a difficult question, which, however, the farmer answered.

It was now the farmer's turn to ask a question but before he did so, he noted with satisfaction that the train was beginning to slow down. He asked the professor: "Fit is't that has ten legs, a lang neb and nae wings, and it's nae a bird and it's nae an insect, and it fussles and it flees?"

"I must confess you have me stumped," acknowledged the professor. "Here's your pound."

"Thank-you," said the farmer, pocketing the note and getting up to leave the train, which had reached his destination.

"Wait a minute!" said the professor. "Before you go you'll have to tell me the answer."

"I dinna ken it either," admitted the farmer. "Here's your fifty pence."

I suggested earlier that the meanness allegation has become a racial one of the English against Scots, although it is obvious that we revert to it frequently ourselves, and usually when among the English. I will now tell a true story about racial ridicule, and perhaps the reader will find some significance in it.

I think it was in the year 1929 that I was walking along Water Lane, a street in Kingston, Jamaica, noted more for rum than for water, when I was stopped by a well-dressed, stout, obviously educated Negro. He appeared to belong to the professional class. He wore a good lightweight suit and a pith helmet or solar topi, a sign in those days of status among Negroes.

He had halted me opposite a large wayside poster advertising petrol—or, as the Jamaicans, along with the Americans, called it, "gas." "What do you think of that?" he asked me, and there was fire smouldering in his eyes.

I looked carefully. The poster consisted of a cartoon of a white couple in tropical clothes, merrily motoring over a hill, with the caption: "Who's that on top with . . . ?" and the name of the petrol. What had aroused my questioner's interest—and obvious annoyance—was the caricature of a Negro boy in the valley, waving up to the white couple, with a grin like a crescent moon or a slice of melon. Had I been in the mood to encourage the stranger in his protest against what he thought was racialism, I ought to have agreed that it was a bit thick.

Nowadays the couple in the car would be, not white, but handsomely coloured. In those days, not many of the black majority of the Jamaicans owned cars or bought petrol, so presumably the poster makers knew their customers. On the other hand, in a country where Negroes abounded.

135

and where many of them had come far from the condition of servitude for which their ancestors had been forcibly transported across the Atlantic from Africa, this was a foolishly racial poster, even for those days, especially in the burlesquing of the grinning Negro boy adopting an adulatory attitude towards the white road hogs. Not to mention the suggestion in the slogan that the whites were permanently "on top."

"I see what you mean," I said to the man eventually, though I was in no mood to start sympathising with him, as he had the sour look of a man with a chip on his shoulder.

"If you care to come along the lane a moment, I'll show you something," I added.

I led him into a pub, or, as the Jamaicans would say, a rum-shop, where I was not unknown. I asked the coloured woman (almost inevitably, she had a Scots name) to bring the calendar out of the back room. She brought it out and laid it on the counter and I asked the Negro to study it.

It was a Lawson Wood cartoon of two Scots in the kilt, with red cheeks and redder noses, knock-kneed at that, and wildly whiskered. One was playing the pipes, and the other was weeping, and there was a puddle, among bits of broken bottle, on the floor. The title was *Lament for the Departed Spirits.*

"Now, you see," I explained to him, "I am a Scotsman, and this sort of thing I come across everywhere I go. You will even find this calendar hanging up in Scotland. Could anything be more racial than that?"

"Ah," he said, "that's all right for you. You've got *protection.*"

I offered him a drink to mollify him, but he announced he was a strict teetotaller, which was perhaps what was really wrong with him. But after he had left, still seething with indignation, I told the coloured woman what it was all about, and she laughed; but we both admitted that the poster was a bit thick.

And after all there is a big difference between a racial joke against Scots, old and wicked as it is, and a racial joke against a really down-trodden and persecuted race. Negroes sometimes try the Scottish trick of turning the joke against its user, but, while we were persecuted as a nation at various times in our history, and persecuted as a race when we began to take what we thought the Treaty of Union entitled us to— a slice of the London pie!—we have never been in the position that the Negro is fighting hard to get out of.

Ought we, following the example of strong Irish nationalists, to object strongly to the Scotch joke and ban the comic Scot from our stages, clubs, and pubs? If we did follow this line to its logical conclusion, there would be almost nothing left to laugh at—and laughter, the psychologists contend, is necessary to man.

And if we knocked out of literature everything one ought not to laugh at, there would be little left of Cervantes, Shakespeare, Sir Walter Scott, Balzac, Charles Dickens or Mark Twain—not to mention the daddy of them all, Rabelais, and his Scottish translator, Urquhart, who put in a lot of extra gags.

To conclude, here is another of our death jokes. It is from Lex McLean's routine as the old maid in a garret: "I once went wi' an undertaker, but I gave him up when he wanted me to join his Christmas club."

If Lex were a Highland chief, he would be the Macabre of Lochaber.

Index

References to illustrations are in italic figures